What others are saying about this book:

"Finding an old buddy may be an easier chore since the release of this book."
THE AMERICAN LEGION Magazine

"A book that can help former service men and women find friends they have served with or locate specific people to substantiate a claim."
DISABLED AMERICAN VETERANS Magazine

"The title of this specialized little niche-filler describes it perfectly. This book lists just about every conceivable private, federal, and state agency that one might contact."
AMERICAN REFERENCE BOOKS ANNUAL 1990,
Vol. 21, Libraries Unlimited, Inc.

"The author has brought together a whole group of options available to those searching for military personnel."
THE GENEALOGICAL HELPER

"I had been looking for a friend for 13 years without success and I found him in a month with the help of this book."
Doug Salyer, Texas

"I have accomplished more with this book in two months than I did in three years on my own. I have found most of my World War II unit."
Howard Ashcraft, Virginia

"This book leaves few stones unturned."
MILITARY REUNION HANDBOOK

And other favorable reviews and articles have been published by VFW, Purple Heart, AMVETS, US Air Force Afterburner, Soldier of Fortune, International Combat Arms, The Retired Officer, Off Duty magazines, and Philadelphia Inquirer and Stars and Stripes newspapers. Listed in "Directories In Print." Also featured on "For Veterans Only" television program on Public Broadcasting Service.

Armed Forces Locator Directory
The book that has helped thousands locate thousands.

Table of Contents

About The Author

Lt. Col. Richard (Dick) S. Johnson served 28 years in the US Army as an enlisted man, as an Armor officer for 10 years, and as a member of the Adjutant General Corps in various personnel and administrative staff positions for 15 years. These positions were concerned with personnel records, and assignments, military postal operations and automated data processing. The latter was involved with the collection of military personnel records on computers and the operation of two Army locators. He retired in December 1979, and received numerous Army decorations for outstanding and meritorious service during his military career.

After retirement from the Army, Dick and his wife Mickey, traveled throughout Europe, Asia, the Near East, Central America and the entire United States.

For the last several years, when not traveling, he has done extensive research on the subject of locating current and former members of the military.

In 1988 Dick authored and published the first edition of *How to Locate Anyone Who is or Has Been in the Military: Armed Forces Locator Directory.* 20,000 copies of this unique book have been sold and it's now in its forth edition. Dick has appeared on numerous TV and radio shows, has been the subject of several newspaper articles and is a frequent speaker on the subject of locating people who have had a military connection. He also does consulting and takes individual cases in locating missing people. Dick has located people for Reunion, the television program, numerous military reunion organizations, attorneys, private investigators and other individuals. He is the foremost authority in the nation on locating people with a military connection.

PREFACE

The purpose of this book is to provide the reader with information on how to locate present or former members of the military. This includes members of the Army, Navy, Air Force, Marine Corps, Coast Guard, the Reserve Components, retired members and former members. Whatever the reason for your search, this book provides the best methods to locate and contact present and former military members. There are many alternative methods that can be used, so it is recommended that you read the entire book before beginning your search.

This book is not designed to find people who have changed their identities and do not want to be found, but rather to locate people who have moved or with whom you have lost contact. There is information regarding debt collection and child support collection that is helpful.

A portion of this book concerns military reunions and veterans organizations. This information is provided to find out about unit reunions. It can also be another method to locate a missing veteran. A great deal of information is provided concerning military records and service numbers. This information is an important source for obtaining units of assignment, date of birth, and service numbers, which in turn can be used to provide a current address.

This book is the only one available that contains this detailed information for this specialized subject. It reflects many years of research and experience that can save you time and expense. Of far greater importance, if you use the information this book contains you will find the person you wish to locate.

This book contains hundreds of telephone numbers, area codes and addresses. Every attempt has been made to insure that all addresses and telephone numbers are correct.

The pronoun "he" is generic as is "serviceman". They refer to both men and women without intending a slight or demeaning attitude toward women service members and veterans.

DEDICATION

This book is dedicated to the 27 million living veterans who have served their country with distinction.

ACKNOWLEDGEMENT

It is impossible to cite all the authorities I have consulted in the preparation of this book. To do so would require more space than is available. The list would include department heads in the Department of Defense, the Department of Veterans Affairs and other federal and state agencies.

I wish to acknowledge the contribution made by Charles Pellegrini, National Personnel Records Center, Dorothy Kennedy formerly of the National Personnel Records Center for unique information on service numbers and records, Alice Hunter, VA Records Processing Center, Paul Valenzuela, Technical Editor, Tom Ninkovich, for editing and outstanding advice, Bill Masciangelo, for support and advice, Gil Gilstrap for endless ideas and my wife Mickey for sound advice and unlimited assistance.

Special acknowledgement is made to the artist of the cover illustration of "The Ghost Troop" by:

Norman Hines
555 Douglas #100
West Sacramento, CA 95605

CHAPTER ONE

SOCIAL SECURITY NUMBER AND SERVICE NUMBER

This chapter provides important information concerning the Social Security number and the military service number. Both of these numbers can be used to obtain the former and current locations of the person you are seeking.

SOCIAL SECURITY NUMBER

The Social Security number, (SSN) is the most important item other than the name of the individual you are trying to locate. Every member of the military, active, reserve, National Guard or retired is identified and listed by his SSN. The same is true for veterans though they can also be listed by their VA claim number or their former service number by the Department of Veteran Affairs (use of military service numbers was discontinued by 1974).

Records in the National Personnel Records Center are identified by SSN except for records received before the SSN replaced the service number, in which case the service numbers are used.

There are several ways you may find a SSN. It is contained on military orders, discharges (DD 214), officers' commissions, and in the Register of Officers published by each military service from 1970 to 1976. Many bank statements contain it as well as some driver's licenses. If you have cancelled checks from the individual they may list the SSN. Personal letters from military members usually have their SSN's included with the return address. All VA claim numbers issued after June 1974 included the veteran's SSN preceded by the letter "C" (example C123456789). You can look at old investments such as money market funds, mutual funds and stock certificates for a SSN. Most department stores ask for a persons SSN when charge accounts are opened. You might get it from schools or places of civilian employment as a civilian. SSN can also be obtained from voter registration information. It will speed your search to know the SSN of the person you are seeking. If you do not know it, the government will not tell you what it is. The Privacy Act of 1974 prohibits the military and federal agencies from giving out this information.

You may need the SSN to have your letters forwarded by the military, Social Security Administration, or the Department of Veterans Affairs. You may also be asked for the SSN when you call an installation locator (see base/post locators chapter two), especially if there is more than one person with the same name. Many times individuals are listed by their SSN because it is easier and quicker to find a number on computer records than trying to find the person by name.

But if you do not have the person's SSN, do not let this stop your search. You may still locate or contact a present or former military member without their SSN if you have one of the following:

a. Name and date of birth.
b. Name and VA claim or file number.
c. Name and former service number.
d. Name and former unit or ship assignment
   (with approximate date assigned).
e. Name and a former address.
f. Name only in some cases.

SOCIAL SECURITY NUMBER PREFIXES

These prefixes indicate the state in which the Social Security number was issued. This will assist you in identifying the state where the individual lived or possibly was born when he obtained his SSN.

001-003	New Hampshire	433-439	Louisiana
004-007	Maine	440-448	Oklahoma
008-009	Vermont	449-467	Texas
010-034	Massachusetts	468-477	Minnesota
035-039	Rhode Island	478-485	Iowa
040-049	Connecticut	486-500	Missouri
050-134	New York	501-502	North Dakota
135-158	New Jersey	503-504	South Dakota
159-211	Pennsylvania	505-508	Nebraska
212-220	Maryland	509-515	Kansas
221-222	Delaware	516-517	Montana
223-231	Virginia	518-519	Idaho
232-236	West Virginia	520	Wyoming
237-246	North Carolina	521-524	Colorado
247-251	South Carolina	525,585	New Mexico
252-260	Georgia	526-527	Arizona
261-267	Florida	528-529	Utah
268-302	Ohio	530	Nevada
303-317	Indiana	531-539	Washington
318-361	Illinois	540-544	Oregon
362-386	Michigan	545-573	California
387-399	Wisconsin	574	Alaska
400-407	Kentucky	575-576	Hawaii
408-415	Tennessee	577-579	Dist Columbia
416-424	Alabama	580	Virgin Islands
425-428	Mississippi	581-586	PR, Guam, AS, PI
		700-729	Railroad

SERVICE NUMBERS

Service numbers for men in the Army were not issued until February 28, 1918, and then only to enlisted men. Officer service numbers were not issued until 1921.

Army service numbers ranged from the numbers 1 through 19,999,999 (8 numerical digits not included in any letter prefix or suffix, see chart 4) until July 1, 1969 when the Social Security account number became the identifying number. The Air Force shared these numbers after its establishment on September 25, 1947, until July 1, 1969, when it also began using Social Security numbers.

During the period 1918 through 1939 Army enlisted service numbers were assigned at random without significance to any geographical area.

Beginning in 1940 each entrance and examining station in the US was allocated certain sets of service numbers for enlisted Army personnel. At times not all numbers were used because of an overestimate of needs in that area.

The US is divided into six Army areas. A set of numbers was allocated to each entrance station identified with that Army area. For example First Army 11,000,000 through 12,999,999 and 31,000,000 through 32,999,999 and 51,000,000 through 51,999,999; Second Army 13,000,000 through 15,999,999 and 52,000,000 through 52,999,999 also 33 and 35 million numbers; Third Army 14 million through 34 million and 53 million ; Fourth Army 18 million through 38 million and 54 million; Fifth Army 16 million through 17 million and 36 million through 37 million and 55 million; Sixth Army 19 million through 39 million and 56 million.

Numbers in the 10 millions and 50 millions were assigned to members who entered outside the Continental US. Numbers in the 21 through 29 millions were assigned to members of the National Guard. (See chart three).

Numbers in the 30 million series were assigned to those men who were inducted (drafted) during WW II. Numbers in the 50 million series were assigned to those who were inducted in the Korean and Vietnam wars.

Late in World War II some men were issued numbers in the 40 million series. Also, some 57 million numbers were issued during the Viet Nam war.

Army officers service numbers never exceeded seven numerical digits plus letter prefix for non-regular officers and six numerical digits plus letter prefix for regular officers (1919 through 1969). See chart four for explanation of prefixes and suffixes to service numbers.

The Navy, Marine Corps and Coast Guard service numbers were different sets of numbers ranging from one digit numbers to seven digit numbers and had no significance as to where they were issued.

TO USE CHARTS ONE, TWO AND THREE

1. To determine when and where a regular (10 through 19 million series) Army or Air Force service number was assigned:
   a. Determine in what state it was issued see chart two.
   b. Next determine what date the service number was issued. See chart one (1940-69).
   Example: 12,250,000 was issued in Delaware or New Jersey (chart two) and was issued between 1946 and 1948.
2. To determine when and where a draftee service number (31 - 37 million and 50 - 57 million) was issued.
   a. Determine which state the service was assigned (chart two).
   b. 31 - 37 million service numbers were assigned between 1940 and 1946.
   c. 51 and 57 million service numbers were assigned between 1948 and 1969.
   Example: A service number 389453400 was issued in Texas, Louisiana, Oklahoma or New Mexico between 1940 and 1946. Service numbers beginning with 50 were assigned in Hawaii, Puerto Rico and Vietnam War (1948-1969).
3. To determine when and where a National Guard service number was assigned:
   a. Determine to which state the service number was assigned (chart three).
   b. Service numbers were utilized from 1940-1969.
   Example: 25914500 was assigned to Texas between 1940 and 1969.

CHART ONE

Service Numbers 10,000,000 thru 19,999,999. These numbers were issued to Regular Air Force and Regular Army Enlisted Men for period indicated below.

10,000,000-10,999,999	1940-1969		
11,000,000-11,142,500	1940-1945	12,000,000-12,242,000	1940-1945
11,142,501-11,188,000	1946-1948	12,242,001-12,321,000	1946-1948
11,166,001-11,238,500	1949-1951	12,321,001-12,393,500	1949-1951
11,238,501-11,283,000	1952-1954	12,393,501-12,469,000	1952-1954
11,283,001-11,344,500	1955-1957	12,469,001-12,553,375	1955-1957
11,344,501-11,384,000	1958-1960	12,553,376-12,614,900	1958-1960
11,384,001-11,999,999	1961-1969	12,614,901-12,999,999	1961-1969
13,000,000-13,197,500	1940-1945	14,000,000-14,204,500	1940-1945
13,197,501-13,299,700	1946-1948	14,204,501-14,300,770	1946-1948
13,299,701-13,408,700	1949-1951	14,300,771-14,454,000	1949-1951
13,408,701-13,511,500	1952-1954	14,454,001-14,547,500	1952-1954
13,511,501-13,621,140	1955-1957	14,547,501-14,661,000	1955-1957
13,621,141-13,705,500	1958-1960	14,661,001-14,745,000	1958-1960
13,705,501-13,999,999	1961-1969	14,745,001-14,999,999	1961-1969
15,000,000-15,201,000	1940-1945	16,000,000-16,201,500	1940-1945
15,201,001-15,280,500	1946-1948	16,201,501-16,307000	1946-1948
15,280,501-15,465,760	1949-1951	16,307,001-16,398,890	1949-1951
15,465,761-15,530,600	1952-1954	16,398,891-16,481,925	1952-1954
15,530,601-15,593,615	1955-1957	16,481,926-16,600,497	1955-1957
15,593,616-15,639,615	1958-1960	16,600,498-16,683,100	1958-1960
15,639,616-15,999,999	1961-1969	16,683,101-16,999,999	1961-1969
17,000,000-17,183,500	1940-1945	18,000,000-18,247,100	1940-1945
17,183,501-17,254,500	1946-1948	18,247,101-18,360,800	1946
17,254,501-17,338,840	1949-1951	18,360,801-18,546,000	1947-1957
17,338,841-17,410,300	1952-1954	18,546,001-18,607,725	1958-1960
17,410,301-17,512,785	1955-1957	18,607,726-18,999,999	1961-1969
17,512,786-17,592,940	1958-1960		
17,592,941-17,999,999	1961-1969		
19,000,000-19,235,500	1940-1945	Series 10,000,000 to 10,999,999 were
19,235,501-19,324,485	1946-1948	used for initial enlistment occurring
19,324,486-19,420,000	1949-1951	outside the continental limits (AK,
19,420,001-19,520,770	1952-1954	HI, PR, Panama).
19,520,771-19,590,665	1955-1957	
19,590,666-19,597,661	1958	
19,597,662-19,999,999	1959-1969	

CHART TWO

This chart shows the breakdown of service numbers assigned to the entrance stations and the State Adjutants General from 1940 - 1969 for Army, and Air Force personnel after its establishment in 1947.

(1)	(2)	(3)	(4)	(5)	(1)	(2)	(3)	(4)	(5)
AL	14	34	24	53	NV	19	39	29	56
AK	19	39	29	5-02	NH	11	31	21	51
AZ	19	39	29	56	NJ	12	32	22	51
AR	18	38	28	54	NM	18	38	28	54
CA	19	39	29	56	NY	12	32	22	51
CO	17	37	27	55	NC	14	34	24	53
CT	11	31	21	51	ND	17	37	27	55
DE	12	32	22	51	OH	15	35	25	52
FL	14	34	24	53	OK	18	38	28	54
ID	19	39	29	56	OR	19	39	29	56
GA	14	34	24	56	PA	13	33	23	52
IL	16	36	26	55	RI	11	31	21	51
IN	15	35	25	52	SC	14	34	24	53
IA	17	37	27	55	SD	17	37	27	55
KS	17	37	27	55	TN	14	34	24	53
KY	15	35	25	52	TX	18	38	28	54
LA	18	38	28	54	UT	19	39	29	56
ME	11	31	21	51	VT	11	31	21	51
MD	13	33	23	52	VA	13	33	23	52
MA	11	31	21	51	WV	15	35	25	52
MI	16	36	26	55	WA	19	39	29	56
MN	17	37	27	55	WI	16	36	26	55
MS	14	34	24	53	WY	17	37	27	55
MO	17	37	27	55	HI	10-1	201	29	50
MT	19	39	29	56	Panama	10-2	302		50-1
NE	17	37	27	55	PR	10-4	304	29	50-1

(1) State(2) Regular Air Force and Army(3) Draftees 1940-1946 (4) National Guard from 1940 on. See chart three for breakdown of service numbers (5) Draftees 1950-1969

CHART THREE

NATIONAL GUARD SERVICE NUMBERS

This chart shows how enlisted (male) National Guard service numbers were allocated to the various State Adjutants General from 1940 to 1969.

	First Army			Second Army	
State	Beginning	Ending	State	Beginning	Ending
CT	21-000-000	21-139-999	DE	21-140-000	21-189-999
ME	21-190-000	21-259-999	DC	22-910-000	22-959-999
MA	21-260-000	21-619-999	KY	23-170-000	23-269-999
NH	21-620-000	21-689-999	MD	23-270-000	23-379-999
NJ	21-690-000	21-899-999	OH	23-380-000	23-729-999
NY	21-900-000	22-699-999	PA	23-730-000	21-259-999
NJ	22-700-000	22-789-999	VA	24-260-000	24-409-999
RI	22-790-000	22-859-999	WV	24-410-000	24-479-999

	Third Army			Fourth Army	
State	Beginning	Ending	State	Beginning	Ending
AL	24-480-000	24-619-999	AK	25-410-000	25-499-999
FL	24-620-000	24-729-999	LA	25-500-000	25-629-999
GA	24-730-000	24-879-999	NM	25-630-000	25-679-999
MS	24-880-000	24-959-999	OK	25-080-000	25-839-999
NC	24-960-000	25-109-999	TX	25-840-000	26-239-999
SC	25-110-000	25-249-999			
TN	25-250-000	25-409-999			

	Fifth Army			Sixth Army	
State	Beginning	Ending	State	Beginning	Ending
CO	26-240-000	26-329-999	AZ	28-040-000	28-089-000
IL	26-330-000	26-329-999	CA	28-090-000	28-639-999
IN	22-960-000	23-169-999	ID	28-640-000	28-709-999
IO	26-780-000	26-919-999	MT	28-710-000	28-759-999
KS	26-920-000	27-000-999	OR	28-770-000	28-909-999
MI	27-010-000	27-339-999	UT	28-910-000	28-969-999
MN	27-340-000	27-449-999	WA	28-970-000	29-029-999
MO	27-500-000	27-659-999	HI	29-030-000	29-149-999
NE	27-660-000	27-729-999	AK	29-240-000	29-249-999
ND	27-730-000	27-789-999	PR	29-120-000	29-239-999
SD	27-790-000	27-849-999	Unused	29-250-000	29-999-999
WI	27-850-000	28-049-999			
WY	28-020-000	28-039-999			

CHART FOUR

The majority of prefixes and suffixes were used with Air Force and Army service numbers. None are known to have been used with Coast Guard service numbers. Marine Corps used "O" to denote officer and "W" to denote enlisted women. Navy used "W" to denote enlisted women. Also, from December 1965 Navy enlisted personnel received six digit numbers with a "B" prefix (B100000 thru B999999). Following the "B" series was the "D" series (D100000 thru D999999). EM and EW are used to show enlisted men and enlisted women.

Character	Used as	Service	Designation
A	prefix	Army	Enlisted women (WAC) without specification of component
A	suffix	Air Force	Used until 1965 for Regular AF male officers
AA	prefix	Air Force	Women enlisted personnel (WAF)
AD	prefix	Air Force	Aviation Cadets
AF	prefix	Air Force	Male enlisted personnel other than aviation cadets
AO	prefix	Air Force	Reserve officers from about 1947-1965
AR	prefix	Air Force	Used until about 1965 for enlisted reserve of the AF and USAF Dieticians
AW	prefix	Air Force	Used from about 1947-1965 for male reserve of the AF and USAF Warrant Officers
E	suffix	Air Force	Used until 1965 for Regular AF male Warrant Officers
ER	prefix	Army	Members of Army Reserve, including those enlisted personnel of Army Nat'l Guard transferred from AUS, RA, or NGUS.
F	prefix	Army	Used with Field Clerks numbers in 800,000 series in WWI
FG	prefix	Air Force	Air National Guard Officers and warrant officers (male and female)
FR	prefix	Air Force	Regular AF officers and warrant officers (male and female)
FR	prefix	Army	Certain Army enlisted reservists from date unknown through October 3, 1962
FT	prefix	Air Force	Officers and warrant officers without component (male and female)
FV	prefix	Air Force	Reserve officers and warrant officers
H	prefix	Air Force	Used until 1965 for regular AF women warrant officers
K	suffix	Air Force	Used until about 1965 for AF academy cadets
K	prefix	Army	Women officers except regular Army with SN,s 100,001 or higher, Army Nurse Corps, Army Medical Specialists Corps, and Women's Army Corps

Character	Used as	Service	Designation
KF	prefix	Army	Regular Army Women officers with service numbers 100,001 and higher
L	prefix	Army	Women's Army Corps (officers)
MJ	prefix	Army	Occupational Therapist Officers
MM	prefix	Army	Physical Therapist Officers
MN	prefix	Army	Male officers of Army Nurse Corps
MR	prefix	Army	Dieticians
N	prefix	Army	Female Nurses (officers)
NG	prefix	Army	Army National Guard enlisted personnel
O	prefix	Army	Male officers except regular Army with SN's 100,001 and higher after October 28, 1963; and Army Nurse Corps and Army Medical Specialists Corps
O	prefix	Mar	Corps Officers
OF	prefix	Army	Regular Army male officers with SN's 100,001 and higher after October 28, 1963
R	prefix	Army	Officer Dieticians
R	prefix	Army	Used on Army WWI EM numbers 1 thru 5,999,999 if man reenlisted
RA	prefix	Army	Regular Army enlisted personnel (used since approximately October 1945)
RM	prefix	Army	Regular Army EM holding appointments as warrant officer in the active Army reserve
RO	prefix	Army	Regular Army enlisted holding commissions in the active Army reserve
RP	prefix	Army	Retired EM recalled to Active Duty now on retired status (used only for those transferred to Retired Army reserve)
RV	prefix	Army	Women's Army Corps Warrant officers holding commissions in active reserves
RW	prefix	Army	Warrant officers holding commissions in active reserves
T	prefix	Army	Flight officers appointed from enlisted ranks number range from T10,000 thru T223,600 (1942 to date unknown)
UR	prefix	Army	Inductees holding commissions or warrants in active Army reserve
US	prefix	Army	Enlisted men without specification of component
V	prefix	Army	Women's Army Corps officers
W	prefix	Army	Warrant officers W prefix Marine Corps Women enlisted personnel
W	suffix	Air Force	Used until 1965 for Regular AF Women commissioned officers
W	suffix	Navy	Women enlisted personal
WA	prefix	Army	Regular Army enlisted women (WAC)
WL	prefix	Army	Regular Army enlisted women holding commissions in the active Army reserve
WM	prefix	Army	Regular Army enlisted women holding warrants in the Army active reserve

Character	Used as	Service	Designation
WR	prefix	Army	Enlisted women reservists (WAC)

Service numbers were discontinued and were replaced by Social Security numbers on the following dates:

Army and Air Force	July 1, 1969
Navy and Marine Corps	July 1, 1972
Coast Guard	Oct. 1, 1974

CHAPTER TWO

HOW TO LOCATE ACTIVE DUTY MILITARY

This chapter describes the ways to locate members of the Armed Forces who are on active duty. The Armed Forces World–Wide Locators, Base and Post locators and Army, Air Force and Fleet Post Offices (APO's and FPO's) provide means to locate active duty members.

ARMED FORCES WORLD –WIDE LOCATORS

The Armed services' World–Wide Locators will either forward a letter or provide you with the current military unit of assignment. The latter may be limited to assignments in the United States.

If you want to have a letter forwarded, place the letter in a sealed, stamped envelope. Put your name and return address in the upper left hand corner. In the center of the envelope put the rank, full name of the service member, followed by the Social Security number (if known). On a separate sheet of paper put everything you know that may help the military locator such as:

Name
Rank
Social Security number
Military service e.g., active Air Force
Date of birth (estimated if actual is unknown)
Sex
Officer or enlisted (if you do not know or not sure of the rank)
Date entered service, Last assignment (if known).

In another envelope, preferably legal size, enclose the letter you want forwarded along with the fact sheet and a check for the search fee (the current search fee for all Armed Forces is $3.50, make check payable to Treasurer of the US). If you are active, reserve, National Guard, retired military or a family member, state it on the fact sheet showing your rank and SSN or relationship, and you will not need to send the search fee. On the outer envelope include your name and return address. Address it to the appropriate locator below. If the military locator can identify the individual in their files it will forward your letter. It is up to the individual to reply to your letter. The military can not require a reply in this process. If the military locator cannot identify the person you are seeking, it will return your letter and tell you why. Common problems include: the locator cannot identify the individual without a SSN and the name is not unique; the individual has been separated from the service; the SSN is incorrect; or the individual is deceased.

To find what unit and military installation a person is assigned, write a letter to the appropriate address below and include as much information as possible that will assist in identifying the person (include the same information as shown above).

If you already know the installation you can call directly to that installation's assistance operator or the installation locator (see instructions under "Base/Post Locator Service" located in this chapter). You can also mail a letter to the individual in care of the installation locator (see list of base/post locators for proper mailing address).

TO LOCATE ACTIVE DUTY
NAVY PERSONNEL

Navy Military Personnel Command   (202) 694-5011
World–Wide Locator   (202) 694-3155
N-0216
Washington, DC 20370

This locator will provide the US land based unit location of all active duty and active reserve personnel over the telephone. If you know the ship the member is assigned see fleet listing in this chapter for correct mailing address.

TO LOCATE ACTIVE DUTY ARMY PERSONNEL

Army World Wide Locator   (317) 542-4211
Ft. Benjamin Harrison, IN 46249-5301
This locator will provide unit of assignment over the phone to family members who provide name and SSN or date of birth of service member.

TO LOCATE ACTIVE DUTY COAST GUARD PERSONNEL

Commandant   (202) 267-1340
US Coast Guard
Locator Service G-PIM-2
2100 2nd Street, S.W.
Washington, DC 20593-0001

The Coast Guard will provide ship or station of assignment and unit telephone number of active duty personnel when requested by telephone. A $5.20 search fee is charged to provide a written verification of unit assignment.

TO LOCATE ACTIVE DUTY MARINE CORPS PERSONNEL

Commandant   (703) 640-3942
Marine Corps (MMRB-10)
Locator Service
Bldg 2008
Quantico, VA 22134-0001

TO LOCATE ACTIVE DUTY AIR FORCE PERSONNEL

USAF World Wide Locator   Recording (512) 652-5774
9504 IH 35 N.   (512) 652-5775
San Antonio, TX 78233-6636

The Air Force locator will forward only one letter per each request and will not provide overseas unit of assignment of active members. Requests for more than one address per letter will be returned without action. Include self-addressed stamped envelope with request for unit assignment. If the individual is separated from the Air Force, they will tell you (1964 to date).

TO LOCATE NATIONAL OCEANIC AND ATMOSPHERIC ADMINISTRATION PERSONNEL

Commissioned Personnel Division   (301) 443-8910
CI N009
Rockville, MD 20852

TO LOCATE US PUBLIC HEALTH SERVICE PERSONNEL

US Public Health Service   (301) 443-3087
Department of Health and Human Services
PHS/CPOD
5600 Fishers Lane
Parklawn Bldg Room 4-35
Rockville, MD 20857

BASE/POST LOCATOR SERVICE

The Armed Services has locator services at most of their installations. The Freedom of Information Act provides that the services may release a military member's unit or ship assignment. They may provide their duty telephone number, but will not give out their SSN or home address, except when the individual has authorized the release of this information. You may need to provide SSN or rank if there is more than one person with the same name. You can call the locator if you know the installation where the person is assigned. Locators normally operate during normal duty hours, usually 7:00 or 7:30 A.M. to 4:00 or 4:30 P.M. Monday through Friday. Locator service is normally provided by a separate office at larger bases. Sometimes it is provided by the Telephone Information Operator or by the Staff Duty Officer after normal working hours and holidays. When you call, give the name and rank of the person you are looking for and ask for their duty assignment, work telephone number, home address and telephone number. Individuals may have authorized release of some addresses and telephone numbers. Many enlisted people live in barracks, dormitories, or quarters on the base as do many single NCO and Officers. They can be contacted through the Charge of Quarters of their unit after normal duty hours. Some married NCO and Officers live on base in quarters and they usually have telephone numbers that are available through the local telephone company. Call the local civilian information operator to find out if they have a listed telephone number. Many military members live in the civilian communities close to the military installation they are assigned. To obtain the telephone number of an installation locator not listed below, you can call the installation information operator to get the number. If you know the unit of the person you are trying to reach, the operator can give you that telephone number. You may also write to the locator to obtain the number. Locators keep forwarding addresses for all personnel who are separated from the service or have been transferred for six months after departure. Mail for personnel who were assigned to decommissioned ships or closed installations will be forwarded for sixty days after closing or decommissioning.

UNIFORMED SERVICES FACILITIES
IN THE UNITED STATES

The following abbreviations are used:

AFB	Air Force Base	NAS	Naval Air Station
AFS	Air Force Station	NS	Naval Station
AMC	Army Medical Center	NSA	Naval Support Activity
ANG	Air National Guard	NSB	Naval Submarine Base
CG	Coast Guard	NSY	Naval Ship Yard
CTR	Center	NWS	Naval Weapons Station
DET	Detachment	PSNL	Personnel
FAC	Facility	SPT	Support
MC	Marine Corps	STN	Station
MSL	Missile	SYS	Systems
NAB	Naval Amphibious Base	TRNG	Training

State/ City	Installation	ZIP Code	Information Number	Locator Number
ALABAMA				
Anniston	Anniston Army Depot	36201	205-235-7501	235-7549
Anniston	Fort McClellan	36205	205-848-4611	848-3795
Birmingham	ANG Base	35217	205-841-9200	841-9200
Dothan	Hall ANG Station	36301	205-792-6793	792-6793
Gadsen	Martin ANG Station	35904	205-442-9700	442-9700
Huntsville	Redstone Arsenal	35898	205-876-2151	876-3331
Mobile	CG Aviation Trng Ctr.	36608	205-694-6110	694-6127
Mobile	CG Base	36615	205-690-3109	690-3109
Montgomery	Dannelly Field	36105	205-284-7100	284-7100
Montgomery	Gunter AFB	36114	205-293-1110	293-5027
Montgomery	Maxwell AFB	36112	205-293-1110	293-5027
Ozark	Fort Rucker	36362	205-255-6181	255-4580
Selma	Craig AFS	36701	205-875-7059	875-7059
ALASKA				
Adak	Naval Station	98791	907-592-8001	592-8001
Anchorage	Elmendorf AFB	99506	907-552-1110	552-4860
Anchorage	Fort Richardson	99505	907-873-1121	873-3255
Anchorage	Kulis ANG Base	99502	907-249-1176	249-1176
Clear	Air Force Station	99704	907-585-6113	585-6113
Delta Junction	Fort Greely	99737	907-873-1121	873-3255
Fairbanks	Eielson AFB	99702	907-377-1110	377-1841
Fairbanks	Fort Wainwright	99703	907-353-7500	353-6586
Juneau	CG Air Station	99801	907-586-7340	586-7340
Ketchikan	CG Base	99901	907-228-0220	228-0220
King Salmon	King Salmon Airport	99613	907-552-1110	552-4860
Kodiak	CG Support Ctr	99697	907-487-5525	487-5267
Shemya	Air Force Base	99501	907-392-3000	392-3000
Sitka	CG Air Station	99835	907-966-5555	966-5555
Galena	Galena Airport	99741	907-552-1110	592-4860
ARIZONA				
Chandler	Williams AFB	85240	602-988-2611	988-5230
Gila Bend	AF Auxiliary Field	85337	602-683-6200	683-6200
Glendale	Luke AFB	85309	602-856-7411	856-6405
Sierra Vista	Fort Huachuca	85613	602-538-7111	538-7111
Tucson	ANG Base	85734	602-573-2210	573-2210
Tucson	Davis-Monthan AFB	85707	602-750-3900	750-3347
Yuma	Army Proving Ground	85365	602-328-2151	328-2151
Yuma	MC Air Station	85369	602-726-2011	726-2011

State/ City	Installation	ZIP Code	Information Number	Locator Number
ARKANSAS				
Blytheville	Eaker AFB	72317	501-762-7000	762-7260
Fort Smith	Fort Chaffee	72905	501-484-2141	484-2933
Jacksonville	Little Rock AFB	72099	501-988-3131	988-6025
N Little Rock	Camp Joseph T Robinson	72118	501-771-5207	771-5207
Pine Bluff	Arsenal	71602	501-543-3000	543-3000
CALIFORNIA				
29 Palms	MC Base	92278	619-368-6000	368-6853
Alameda	CG Support Center	94501	415-437-3151	437-3151
Alameda	Naval Air Station	94501	415-869-0111	869-0111
Atwater	Castle AFB	95342	209-726-2011	726-4848
Barstow	Ft. Irwin	92310	619-386-4111	386-3369
Barstow	MC Logistical Base	92311	619-577-6211	577-6444
China Lake	Naval Weapons Center	93555	619-939-2303	939-9011
Concord	Naval Weapon Station	94520	415-246-2000	246-5040
Coronado	NAB	92155	619-522-5000	522-5000
Coronado	North Island NAS	92135	619-524-0444	524-0444
Costa Mesa	ANG Station	92627	714-979-1343	979-1343
El Centro	Naval Air Facility	92243	619-339-2555	339-2468
Fairfield	Travis AFB	94535	707-424-5000	424-2026
Herlong	Sierra Army Depot	96113	916-827-4000	827-4328
Jolon	Fort Hunter Liggett	93928	408-385-5911	385-2520
Lancaster	Edwards AFB	93523	805-277-1110	277-2777
Lathrop	Sharpe Army Depot	95331	209-982-2011	982-2011
Lemoore	Naval Air Station	93245	209-998-2211	998-3059
Lompoc	Vandenberg AFB	93437	805-866-1611	866-1841
Long Beach	Naval Station	90822	213-547-6721	547-6721
Long Beach	Seal Beach NWS	90740	213-594-7011	594-7101
Los Alamitos	Armed Forces Reserve Ctr.	90720	213-493-8000	493-8000
Los Angeles	Air Force Base	90009	213-643-1000	643-1876
Mare Island	Naval Station	94592	707-646-1111	646-3354
Marysville	Beale AFB	95903	916-634-3000	634-2657
Monterey	Fort Ord	93941	408-242-2211	242-2271
Monterey	Naval Postgraduate School	93943	408-646-2441	646-2441
Monterey	Presidio of Monterey	93940	408-647-5000	647-5000
Oakland	Naval Hospital	94627	415-633-5000	633-5000
Oakland	Naval Supply Center	94625	415-466-0112	395-3491
Oakland	Oakland Army Base	94626	415-466-9111	466-2839
Oceanside	Camp Pendleton	92055	619-725-4111	725-4111
Petaluma	CG Trng Ctr	94952	707-765-7212	765-7380
Point Arena	Point Arena AFS	95468	707-882-2165	882-2165
Point Mugu	Naval Air Station	93042	805-989-1110	989-8523
Point Mugu	Pacific Missile Test Ctr	93042	805-989-1110	989-8523
Port Hueneme	Naval Const Bn Ctr	93043	805-982-4571	982-4711

State/ City	Installation	ZIP Code	Information Number	Locator Number

CALIFORNIA (Cont.)

State/ City	Installation	ZIP Code	Information Number	Locator Number
Riverside	March AFB	92518	714-655-1110	655-4648
Sacramento	Army Depot	95813	916-388-2211	388-2211
Sacramento	Mather AFB	95655	916-364-1110	364-2597
Sacramento	McClellan AFB	95652	916-643-2111	643-6443
San Bernardino	Norton AFB	92409	714-382-1110	382-5381
San Diego	CG Air Station	92101	619-557-5870	557-6510
San Diego	MC Recruit Depot	92140	619-524-1720	524-1719
San Diego	Miramar NAS	92145	619-537-1011	537-6018
San Diego	Naval Station	92136	619-556-1011	556-1011
San Diego	Naval Hospital	92134	619-532-6400	532-6400
San Diego	Naval Submarine Base	92106	619-553-8663	553-8663
San Diego	Naval Trng. Center	92133	619-524-1011	524-4623
San Francisco	Treasure Island NSA	94130	415-765-6411	395-3491
San Francisco	Presidio of San Francisco	94129	415-561-2211	561-4345
San L. Obispo	Camp San L. Obispo	93403	805-549-3800	549-3800
San Miguel	Camp Roberts	93451	805-238-3100	238-3100
San Pedro	CG Personnel Center	90731	213-514-6402	514-6402
Santa Ana	MC Air Station El Toro	92709	714-726-2100	726-3736
Stockton	Naval Comm. Station	95203	209-944-0284	944-7284
Sunnyvale	Onizuka AFB	94088	415-966-5628	966-5628
Sunnyvale	Moffett Field NAS	94035	415-966-5411	966-4887
Tracy	Defense Depot	95376	209-832-9000	832-9000
Vallejo	Mare Island Naval Station	94592	707-646-1111	646-2115
Victorville	George AFB	92394	619-269-1110	269-3208

COLORADO

State/ City	Installation	ZIP Code	Information Number	Locator Number
Aurora	Buckley ANG Base	80010	303-340-9447	340-9447
Aurora	Fitzsimmons AMC	80045	303-361-8241	361-8802
Colo. Springs	Air Force Academy	80840	719-472-3110	472-3110
Colo. Springs	Falcon AFS	80912	719-550-4113	550-4020
Colo. Springs	Fort Carson	80913	719-579-5811	579-3341
Colo. Springs	Peterson AFB	80914	719-554-7321	554-4020
Denver	Lowry AFB	80230	303-370-1110	370-4171
Pueblo	Army Depot	81001	719-549-4111	549-4111
Rocky Mt	Rocky Mt Arsenal	80240	303-288-0711	289-0200

CONNECTICUT

State/ City	Installation	ZIP Code	Information Number	Locator Number
East Granby	Bradley ANG Base	06026	203-623-8291	623-8291
Groton	New London NSB	06340	203-449-3011	449-3709
New Haven	Long Island Sound CG	06512	203-773-2401	773-2401
New London	US Coast Guard Academy	06320	203-444-8444	444-8444
Orange	Orange ANG Comm. Stn.	06477	203-795-4786	795-4786

State/ City	Installation	ZIP Code	Information Number	Locator Number

DELAWARE

Dover	Dover AFB	19902	302-677-2113	677-2841

DISTRICT OF COLUMBIA

Washington	Andrews AFB	20331	301-981-9111	981-6161
Washington	Bolling AFB	20332	202-545-6700	767-4522
Washington	Coast Guard HQ	20593	202-267-2229	267-1340
Washington	Fort McNair	20319	202-545-6700	475-2005
Washington	Marine Barracks	20003	202-433-4073	694-3344
Washington	Marine Corps HQ	20380	202-694-1913	694-3344
Washington	National Guard Bureau	20310	703-697-4841	697-4841
Washington	Navy Yard	20374	202-545-6700	433-2037
Washington	Pentagon	20310	703-545-6700	545-6700
Washington	Walter Reed AMC	20307	202-576-3501	576-3767

FLORIDA

Avon Park	Air Force Range	33825	813-452-4114	452-4114
Cape Canave.	Cape Canaveral AFS	32925	407-853-1110	494-4542
Clearwater	CG Air Station	34622	813-535-1437	535-1437
Cocoa Beach	Patrick AFB	32925	407-494-1110	494-4542
Crestview	Duke Field AFS	32542	904-882-1110	882-1110
Cuedjoe Keys	Cuedjoe Keys AFS	33044	305-292-3121	292-3121
Ft. Walton Bch	Eglin AFB	32542	904-881-6668	882-4478
Ft. Walton Bch	Hurlburt Field	32544	904-881-6668	882-6333
Homestead	Homestead AFB	33039	305-257-8011	257-7621
Jacksonville	Naval Air Station	32212	904-772-2338	772-2340
Jacksonville	NAS Cecil Field	32215	904-778-5626	778-5240
Key West	Naval Air Station	33040	305-292-2434	292-2256
Mayport	CG Base	32267	904-247-7301	247-7301
Mayport	Naval Station	32228	904-246-5401	246-5401
Miami	Seventh CG District	33131	305-536-5632	536-5632
Miami	CG Base	33139	305-535-4300	535-4300
Milton	NAS Whiting Field	32570	904-623-7437	623-7437
Opa-Locka	CG Air Station Miami	33054	305-953-2100	953-2100
Orlando	Naval Training Center	32813	407-646-4111	646-5366
Panama City	Naval Coastal Sys Ctr	32407	904-234-4011	234-4378
Panama City	Tyndall AFB	32403	904-283-1113	283-2138
Pensacola	Naval Air Tech Trng Ctr	32508	904-452-0111	452-4698
Pensacola	Corry Naval Station	32511	904-452-2000	452-4693
Pensacola	Naval Hospital	32512	904-452-6601	452-6601
Pensacola	Shufley Field	32509	904-4520111	452-4698
St. Petersburg	CG Station	33701	813-893-3454	893-3454
Starke	Camp Blanding	32091	904-533-3100	533-3100
Tampa	MacDill AFB	33608	813-830-1110	830-2444

State/ City	Installation	ZIP Code	Information Number	Locator Number

GEORGIA

State/City	Installation	ZIP Code	Information Number	Locator Number
Albany	MC Logistic Base	31704	912-439-5000	439-5103
Athens	Naval Supply School	30606	404-354-1500	354-1500
Atlanta	Fort McPherson	30330	404-752-3113	752-2743
Augusta	Fort Gordon	30905	404-791-0110	791-4675
Columbus	Fort Benning	31905	404-544-1011	545-5216
Dahlonega	Camp Merrill	30533	404-545-2415	545-2415
Forest Park	Fort Gillem	30050	404-363-5000	752-2743
Hinesville	Fort Stewart	31314	912-767-1110	767-2862
Kings Bay	Naval Submarine Base	31547	912-673-2000	673-2160
Marietta	Atlanta NAS	30060	404-421-5503	421-5354
Marietta	Dobbins AFB	30069	404-421-5000	421-4529
Savannah	Hunter Army Airfield	31409	912-352-6521	767-2862
Valdosta	Moody AFB	31699	912-333-4211	333-3585
Warner Robins	Robins AFB	31098	912-926-1110	926-6027

HAWAII

State/City	Installation	ZIP Code	Information Number	Locator Number
Barbers Point	Naval Air Station	96862	808-471-7110	684-1005
Honolulu	Camp HM Smith USMC	96861	808-471-7110	477-5106
Honolulu	Fort Shafter	96858	808-471-7110	438-2484
Honolulu	Tripler Army Med Ctr	96859	808-471-7110	438-2484
Honolulu	Hickam AFB	96853	808-471-7110	449-0165
Honolulu	Sand Is CG Base	96819	808-541-0111	541-0001
Kaneohe Bay	Kaneohe MC Air Station	96863	808-471-7110	257-2008
Kekaha	Barking Sands Pacific Missile Range (Navy)	96752	808-471-7110	474-6249
Pearl Harbor	Naval Base	96860	808-471-7110	474-6249
Wahiawa	Naval Ammo Area	96786	808-471-7110	474-6249
Wahiawa	Schofield Barracks	96857	808-471-7110	438-2484
Wahiawa	Wheeler AFB	96854	808-471-7110	449-0165
Wahiawa	Kunia Field Station	96819	808-471-7110	474-6249
Waianae	Lualualei Naval Magazine	96792	808-471-7110	474-6249
Waianae	Army Recreation Center	96792	808-471-7110	438-2484
Waimanalo	Bellows AFS	96853	808-471-7110	449-0165

IDAHO

State/City	Installation	ZIP Code	Information Number	Locator Number
Boise	Gowen Field ANG Base	83707	208-389-5011	389-5011
Mountain Hm.	Mountain Home AFB	83648	208-828-2111	828-6647

ILLINOIS

State/City	Installation	ZIP Code	Information Number	Locator Number
Belleville	Scott AFB	62225	618-256-1110	256-1841
Chicago	O'Hare Air Res. Facility	60666	312-694-6000	694-6000
Glenview	Glenview NAS	60026	708-657-1000	657-2303

State/ City	Installation	ZIP Code	Information Number	Locator Number

ILLINOIS (Cont.)

State/City	Installation	ZIP Code	Information Number	Locator Number
Granite City	Price Support Center	62040	618-452-4212	452-4212
Great Lakes	Naval Training Center	60088	708-688-3939	688-2014
Highland Park	Fort Sheridan	60037	708-926-4111	926-2274
Moline	Rock Island Arsenal	61299	309-782-1110	782-1110
Rantoul	Chanute AFB	61868	217-495-1110	495-3545

INDIANA

State/City	Installation	ZIP Code	Information Number	Locator Number
Crane	Naval Weapon Spt Ctr	47522	812-854-2511	854-2511
Edinburgh	Camp Atterburg	46124	812-526-9711	526-9711
Indianapolis	Fort Benjamin Harrison	46216	317-546-9211	542-4537
Indianapolis	Naval Avionics Ctr	46219	317-359-8471	359-8471
Madison	Jefferson ProvingGround	47250	812-273-7211	273-7211
Peru	Grissom AFB	46971	317-689-5211	689-3032

IOWA

State/City	Installation	ZIP Code	Information Number	Locator Number
Des Moines	ANG Base	50321	515-287-9210	287-9210

KANSAS

State/City	Installation	ZIP Code	Information Number	Locator Number
Junction City	Fort Riley	66442	913-239-3911	239-9867
Leavenworth	Fort Leavenworth	66027	913-684-4021	684-3651
Topeka	Forbes Field ANG Base	66620	913-862-1234	862-1234
Wichita	McConnell AFB	67221	316-652-6100	652-3555

KENTUCKY

State/City	Installation	ZIP Code	Information Number	Locator Number
Fort Knox	Fort Knox	40121	502-624-1181	624-1141
Hopkinsville	Fort Campbell	42223	502-798-2151	798-7196
Lexington	Lexington-Blue Grass Army Depot	40511	606-293-3011	293-3126

LOUISIANA

State/City	Installation	ZIP Code	Information Number	Locator Number
Alexandria	England AFB	71301	318-448-2100	448-5314
Bossier City	Barksdale AFB	71110	318-456-2252	456-3555
Hammond	Hammond ANG Com Stn	70401	207-772-2018	772-2018
Leesville	Fort Polk	71459	318-535-2911	535-6523
New Orleans	CG Support Center	70117	504-942-3020	942-3020
New Orleans	Jackson Barracks	70146	504-271-6262	271-6262
New Orleans	Naval Air Station	70143	504-393-3253	393-3253
New Orleans	Naval Support Activity	70142	504-948-5011	361-2762
Pineville	Camp Beauregard	71360	318-640-2080	640-2080

State/ City	Installation	ZIP Code	Information Number	Locator Number

MAINE

State/ City	Installation	ZIP Code	Information Number	Locator Number
Augusta	Camp Keyes	04333	207-622-9331	622-9331
Bangor	ANG Base	04401	207-947-0571	990-7508
Brunswick	Naval Air Station	04011	207-921-2214	924-3155
Bucks	Harbor AFS	04618	207-255-8316	255-8316
East Machias	Naval Radio Station	04630	207-259-8218	259-8218
Limestone	Caswell AFS	04750	207-999-1110	999-1110
Limestone	Loring AFB	04751	207-999-1110	999-2100
Presque Is.	AFS	04769	207-764-5195	764-5195
South Portland	CG Base	04106	207-767-0302	767-0333
Winter Harbor	Naval Security Group	04693	207-963-5534	963-5534

MARYLAND

State/ City	Installation	ZIP Code	Information Number	Locator Number
Aberdeen	Aberdeen Proving Ground	21005	301-278-5201	278-5138
Aberdeen	Edgewood Arsenal	21005	301-278-5201	278-5138
Annapolis	US Naval Academy/NS	21402	301-267-6100	267-3898
Baltimore	Fort Ritchie	21719	301-878-1300	878-5685
Bethesda	National Naval Med Ctr	20814	202-295-1246	295-2896
Camp Springs	Andrews AFB	20331	301-981-9111	981-6161
Curtis Bay	CG Yard	21226	301-789-1600	789-1600
Frederick	Fort Detrick	21701	301-663-8000	663-2233
Indian Head	Naval Ordnance Station	20640	301-743-4000	743-4000
Odenton	Fort George G. Meade	20755	301-677-6261	677-4547
Patuxent River	Naval Air Station	20670	301-863-3000	863-1097
Solomons	Navy Recreation Center	20688	301-326-4216	326-4217

MASSACHUSETTS

State/ City	Installation	ZIP Code	Information Number	Locator Number
Ayer	Fort Devens	01433	508-796-3911	796-2748
Bedford	Hanscom AFB	01731	617-377-4441	377-5111
Boston	CG Support Ctr	02109	617-223-3257	223-3257
Chicopee	Westover AFB	01022	413-557-1110	557-3874
Mil. Res.	Camp Edwards	02542	508-968-5885	968-5885
Natick	Army R & D Eng Ctr	01760	508-651-4300	651-4300
Otis	Cape Cod AFS	02542	508-968-1000	968-1000
Otis	ANG Base	02542	508-968-1000	968-4181
Otis	CG Air Station	02542	508-968-5300	968-1667
S. Boston	CG Support Acty	02210	617-223-3257	223-3257
S. Weymouth	Naval Air Station	02190	617-786-2500	786-2605
Watertown	Army Research Ctr	02172	617-923-5000	923-5000
Westfield	Bornes M. Airport	01085	413-568-9151	568-9151
Worcester	Worcester ANG Base	01605	508-792-5711	799-6963

State/ City	Installation	ZIP Code	Information Number	Locator Number

MICHIGAN

State/ City	Installation	ZIP Code	Information Number	Locator Number
Alpena	Collins ANG Base	49707	517-354-6550	354-6550
Calument	AFS	49913	906-337-4200	337-4200
Detroit	CG Group	48207	313-568-9524	568-9524
Grand Haven	CG Group	49417	616-847-4500	847-4517
Grayling	Camp Grayling	49739	517-348-7621	348-7621
Gwinn KI	Sawyer AFB	49843	906-346-6511	346-2605
Muskegon	CG Group	49441	616-759-8684	759-8684
Oscoda	Wurtsmith AFB	48753	517-739-2011	747-6582
Port Austin	AFS	48467	517-738-5111	738-5111
Selfridge	Selfridge ANG Base	48045	313-466-4011	466-4021
S. St Marie	CG Base	49783	906-635-3217	635-3217
Traverse City	CG Air Station	49684	616-922-8214	922-8214
Warren	Detroit Arsenal	48090	313-573-1000	573-1000

MINNESOTA

State/ City	Installation	ZIP Code	Information Number	Locator Number
Little Falls	Camp Ripley	56345	612-632-6631	632-6631
Minneapolis	MSP Intr Airport	55417	612-725-5011	725-5011

MISSISSIPPI

State/ City	Installation	ZIP Code	Information Number	Locator Number
Bay S. Louis	Naval Oceanography	39529	601-688-2211	688-2211
Biloxi	Keesler AFB	39534	601-377-1110	377-2798
Columbus	Columbus AFB	39701	601-434-7322	434-2841
Gulfport	Naval Const Bn Ctr	39501	601-865-2555	865-2121
Hattiesburg	Camp Shelby	39407	601-584-2000	584-2000
Jackson	Thompson Field	39205	601-939-3633	939-3633
Meridian	Naval Air Station	39309	601-679-2211	679-2301

MISSOURI

State/ City	Installation	ZIP Code	Information Number	Locator Number
Grandview	Richards-Gebaur AFB	64030	816-348-2132	348-2132
Knob Noster	Whiteman AFB	65305	816-687-1110	687-3201
St. Louis	Army Res Psnl Ctr	63132	800-325-8311	325-8311
St. Louis	CG Base	63111	314-425-6800	425-6800
Waynesville	Fort Leonard Wood	65473	314-368-0113	368-2151

MONTANA

State/ City	Installation	ZIP Code	Information Number	Locator Number
Great Falls	Malmstrom AFB	59402	406-731-1110	731-4121

NEBRASKA

State/ City	Installation	ZIP Code	Information Number	Locator Number
Omaha	Offutt AFB	68113	402-294-1110	294-5125

State/ City	Installation	ZIP Code	Information Number	Locator Number

NEVADA

State/ City	Installation	ZIP Code	Information Number	Locator Number
Fallon	Naval Air Station	89406	702-426-5161	426-2709
Las Vegas	Air Force Auxiliary Field	89191	702-652-0201	652-0401
Las Vegas	Nellis AFB	89191	702-652-1110	652-1841

NEW HAMPSHIRE

State/ City	Installation	ZIP Code	Information Number	Locator Number
Portsmouth	Naval Shipyard	03804	207-438-1000	438-2208
Portsmouth	Pease AFB	03803	603-430-2571	430-1841

NEW JERSEY

State/ City	Installation	ZIP Code	Information Number	Locator Number
Bayonne	Military Ocean Terminal	07202	201-823-5111	823-0111
Cape May	CG Training Center	08204	609-884-6900	884-6910
Center	Picatinny Arsenal	07806	201-724-4021	724-4021
Colts Neck	Earle NWS	07722	201-577-2000	577-2000
Gibbsboro	Gibbsboro AFS	08026	609-783-1449	783-1449
Lakehurst	Naval Air Eng Ctr	08733	201-323-2011	323-2582
Red Bank	Fort Monmouth	07703	201-532-9000	532-1492
Wrightstown	Fort Dix	08640	609-562-1011	562-6051
Wrightstown	McGuire AFB	08641	609-724-1110	724-4288

NEW MEXICO

State/ City	Installation	ZIP Code	Information Number	Locator Number
Alamogordo	Holloman AFB	88330	505-479-6511	479-7510
Albuquerque	Kirtland AFB	87117	505-844-0011	844-0011
Clovis	Cannon AFB	88103	505-784-3311	784-2424
Las Cruces	White Sands MSL Range	88002	505-678-2121	678-1630
Gallup	Ft Wingate Army Depot	87301	505-488-4811	488-5411

NEW YORK

State/ City	Installation	ZIP Code	Information Number	Locator Number
Brooklyn	CG Air Station	11234	718-615-2422	615-2410
Brooklyn	Fort Hamilton	11252	718-630-4101	630-4958
Brooklyn	Naval Station New York	11251	718-834-2000	834-2480
Buffalo	CG Group	14203	716-846-4152	846-4152
Flushing	Fort Totten	11359	718-352-5700	352-5700
Garden City	Mitchell Field NSA	11530	516-222-1285	222-1285
Governors Is.	CG Base	10004	212-668-7000	668-6465
Newburgh	Stewart Army Sub Post	12550	914-563-3000	938-3320
Niagara Falls	Air Force Reserve Base	14304	716-236-2000	236-2000
Plattsburgh	Plattsburgh AFB	12903	518-565-5000	565-5579
Rome	Griffiss AFB	13441	315-330-1110	330-2231
Romulus	Seneca Army Depot	14541	607-869-1110	869-1398
Roslyn	Roslyn ANG Station	11576	516-621-9120	621-9120
Staten Island	Naval Station	11305	718-390-3700	390-3700

State/City	Installation	ZIP Code	Information Number	Locator Number

NEW YORK (Cont.)

State/City	Installation	ZIP Code	Information Number	Locator Number
Staten Island	Fort Wadsworth	10305	718-390-3700	390-3700
Watertown	Fort Drum	13602	315-772-6900	772-5869
Watervlet	Arsenal	12189	518-266-1110	266-1110
West Point	US Military Academy	10996	914-938-4011	938-3910

NORTH CAROLINA

State/City	Installation	ZIP Code	Information Number	Locator Number
Atlantic Beach	Fort Macon CG	28512	919-247-4598	247-4519
Badin	Badin ANG Station	28009	704-422-3617	422-3617
Buxton	Cape Hatteras CG Group	27920	919-995-5881	995-5881
Charlotte	Douglas M. Airport	28219	704-391-4100	391-4100
Cherry Point	MC Air Station	28533	919-466-4232	466-2917
Elizabeth City	CG Support Center	27909	919-338-3941	338-3941
Fayetteville	Fort Bragg	28307	919-396-0011	396-1461
Fayetteville	Pope AFB	28308	919-394-0001	394-4822
Goldsboro	Seymour Johnson AFB	27531	919-736-5400	736-5584
Jacksonville	MC Camp Lejeune	28542	919-451-1113	451-3074
Jacksonville	New River MC Air Station	28545	919-451-6197	451-6554
Kure Beach	Fort Fisher AFS	28449	919-458-6742	458-6742

NORTH DAKOTA

State/City	Installation	ZIP Code	Information Number	Locator Number
Cavalier	Cavalier AFS	58220	701-993-3297	993-3297
Fargo	Hector Field	58102	701-241-8168	241-8168
Grand Forks	Grand Forks AFB	58205	701-747-3000	747-3344
Minot	Minot AFB	58705	701-723-1110	723-1841

OHIO

State/City	Installation	ZIP Code	Information Number	Locator Number
Cincinnati	Blue Ash ANG Station	45242	513-791-7410	791-7410
Cleveland	CG Marine Safety Office	44114	216-522-4405	522-3929
Cleveland	Navy Finance Ctr	44199	800-321-1080	321-1080
Columbus	Rickenbacker ANG Base	43217	614-492-8211	492-3541
Columbus	Def Const Supply Ctr	43216	614-238-2131	238-2131
Dayton	Gentile Supply Depot	45444	513-296-6041	296-6041
Dayton	Wright Patterson AFB	45433	513-257-1110	257-3231
Newark	Air Force Station	43057	614-522-2171	522-7281
Port Clinton	Camp Perry ANG Station	43452	419-635-4021	635-4021

OKLAHOMA

State/City	Installation	ZIP Code	Information Number	Locator Number
Altus	Altus AFB	73523	405-481-8100	481-6402
Braggs	Camp Gruber	74423	918-487-6001	487-6001
Enid	Vance AFB	73701	405-237-2121	249-7791
Lawton	Fort Sill	73503	405-351-8111	351-4052

State/ City	Installation	ZIP Code	Information Number	Locator Number

OKLAHOMA (Cont.)

McAlester	Army Ammo Plant	74501	918-421-2529	421-2529
Oklah'a City	Oklahoma City AFS	73145	405-732-7321	734-2456
Oklah'a City	Tinker AFB	73145	405-732-7321	734-2456

OREGON

Eugene	North Bend CG Air Stn	97459	503-756-9258	756-9258
Klamath Falls	Kingsley Field	97603	503-885-6365	885-6365
Portland	Personnel Support Det.	97217	503-285-3782	285-3782
Warrenton	Camp Riley	97146	503-861-3835	861-3835

PENNSYLVANIA

Annville	Ft. Indiandtown GAP	17003	717-865-5444	865-5444
Carlisle	Carlisle Barracks	17013	717-245-3131	245-1131
Chambersb'g	Letterkenny Army Depot	17201	717-267-8111	267-8111
Horsham	Willow Grove NAS	19090	215-443-1000	443-1000
Mechanicsb'g	Defense Depot	17055	717-790-2000	790-2000
Mechanicsb'g	Naval Ships Parts Ctr	17055	717-790-2000	790-3778
N. Cumberl'd	Army Depot	17070	717-770-6011	770-6011
Oakdale	Kelley Support Ctr	15071	412-777-1173	777-1173
Philadelphia	Defense Psnl Support Ctr	19101	215-952-2000	952-2214
Philadelphia	Naval Avn. Supply Office	19111	215-697-4000	697-4000
Philadelphia	Naval Base	19112	215-897-5000	897-8888
Tobyhanna	Army Depot	18466	717-894-7000	894-7545
Warminster	Naval Air Dev. Ctr	18974	215-441-2000	441-2000

PUERTO RICO

Aguadilla	CG Air Station Borinquen	00604	809-882-3500	882-3500
Ceiba	Roosevelt Road NAS	00635	809-865-2000	865-2000
Sabana Seca	Naval Security Group	00749	809-795-2255	795-2255
Salinas	Camp Santiago	00751	809-824-3110	824-3110
San Juan	CG Base	00903	809-729-6800	729-6800
San Juan	Fort Buchanan	00934	809-783-2424	783-8293

RHODE ISLAND

Davisville	Naval Const Bn Ctr	02854	401-267-2501	267-2501
Newport	Naval Edc and Trng Ctr	02841	401-841-2311	841-4040
Providence	Cranston ANG Station	02910	401-277-2701	277-2701

State/ City	Installation	ZIP Code	Information Number	Locator Number

SOUTH CAROLINA

State/City	Installation	ZIP Code	Information Number	Locator Number
Beaufort	MC Air Station	29904	803-522-7100	522-7188
Beaufort	Naval Hospital	29902	803-525-5600	525-5600
Charleston	Charleston AFB	29404	803-554-0230	554-2669
Charleston	CG Base	29401	803-724-7600	724-7600
Charleston	Naval Base	29408	803-743-4111	743-4111
Charleston	Naval Weapons Station	29408	803-743-4111	743-4111
Columbia	Fort Jackson	29207	803-751-7601	751-7671
Eastover	McEntire ANG Base	29044	803-776-5121	776-5121
Myrtle Beach	Myrtle Beach AFB	29579	803-238-7211	238-7056
Parris Island	MC Recruit Depot	29905	803-525-2111	525-3358
Sumter	Shaw AFB	29152	803-668-8110	668-2166

SOUTH DAKOTA

State/City	Installation	ZIP Code	Information Number	Locator Number
Rapid City	Ellsworth AFB	57706	605-385-1000	385-1379

TENNESSEE

State/City	Installation	ZIP Code	Information Number	Locator Number
Alcoa	Alcoa ANG Station	37701	615-970-3065	970-3065
Knoxville	McGhee Tyson ANG Base	37642	615-970-8200	970-8254
Memphis	Defense Depot	38114	901-775-6011	775-6011
Millington	Memphis NAS	38054	901-873-5111	873-5875
Nashville	ANG	37204	615-252-3001	252-3001
Tullahoma	Arnold AFB	37389	615-454-3000	454-7274

TEXAS

State/City	Installation	ZIP Code	Information Number	Locator Number
Abilene	Dyess AFB	79607	915-696-0212	696-3098
Austin	Bergstrom AFB	78743	512-479-4100	479-1110
Bastrop	Camp Swift	78602	512-321-2497	321-2497
Beeville	Chase Field - NAS	78103	512-354-5119	354-5119
Corpus Christi	Army Depot	78419	512-939-2811	939-2383
Corpus Christi	Naval Air Station	78419	512-939-2811	939-2383
Dallas	Naval Air Station	75211	214-266-6111	266-6640
Del Rio	Laughlin AFB	78840	512-298-3511	298-5195
El Paso	Fort Bliss	79916	915-568-2121	568-1113
Fort Worth	Carswell AFB	76127	817-782-5000	782-7082
Galveston	CG Base	77553	409-766-5623	766-5619
Garland	Garland ANG Station	75040	214-276-0521	276-0521
Houston	Ellington AFB	77209	713-929-2110	929-2110
Killeen	Fort Hood	76544	817-287-1110	287-2137
Kingsville	Naval Air Station	78363	512-595-6136	595-6136
La Porte	La Porte ANG Station	77571	713-471-5111	471-5111
Lubbock	Reese AFB	79489	806-885-4511	885-3678
Nederland	Nederland ANG Station	77627	409-727-2336	727-2336

State/ City	Installation	ZIP Code	Information Number	Locator Number

TEXAS (Cont.)

State/City	Installation	ZIP Code	Information Number	Locator Number
San Angelo	El Dorado AFS	76936	915-654-4000	654-4265
San Angelo	Goodfellow AFB	76908	915-657-3231	654-3410
San Antonio	Brooks AFB	78235	512-536-1110	536-1841
San Antonio	Fort Sam Houston	78234	512-221-1211	221-3302
San Antonio	Lackland AFB	78236	512-671-1110	671-1841
San Antonio	Kelly AFB	78241	512-925-1110	925-1841
San Antonio	Randolph AFB	78150	512-652-1110	652-1841
Texarkana	Red River Army Depot	75507	214-334-2141	334-2726
Wichita Falls	Sheppard AFB	76311	817-676-2511	676-1841

UTAH

State/City	Installation	ZIP Code	Information Number	Locator Number
Dugway	Dugway Proving Ground	84022	801-831-3545	831-2151
Ogden	Hill AFB	84056	801-777-7221	777-1841
Ogden	Defense Depot	84407	801-399-7011	399-7011
Salt Lake City	Camp W G Williams	84065	801-524-3727	524-3727
Salt Lake City	Fort Douglas	84113	801-524-4137	524-4137
Tooele	Army Depot	84074	801-833-3211	883-3211

VIRGINIA

State/City	Installation	ZIP Code	Information Number	Locator Number
Alexandria	Cameron Station	22304	202-545-6700	545-6700
Alexandria	CG Info Sys Ctr	22310	703-644-3600	644-3640
Alexandria	Fort Belvoir	22060	703-664-6071	664-3096
Arlington	Fort Myer	22211	202-545-6700	545-6700
Arlington	Henderson Hall	22214	202-545-6700	694-2344
Blackstone	Fort Pickett	23824	804-292-8621	292-2266
Bowling Gr'n	Fort AP Hill	22427	804-633-5041	633-5041
Charlottesv'le	JAG School	22903	804-972-6300	972-6300
Chesap'k Bay	Naval Security Group	23322	804-421-8000	421-8000
Dahlgren	Naval Surface Warfare Ctr	22448	703-663-8294	663-8294
Hampton	Fort Monroe	23651	804-727-2111	727-2111
Hampton	Langley AFB	23665	804-764-9990	764-5615
Newport N's	Fort Eustis	23604	804-878-1212	878-5215
Norfolk	Little Creek NAB	23521	804-464-7000	464-7602
Norfolk	Naval Station	23511	804-444-0000	444-0000
Petersburg	Fort Lee	23801	804-734-1011	734-2021
Portsmouth	CG Support Center	23703	804-483-8540	483-8540
Portsmouth	Naval Hospital	23708	804-398-5008	398-5624
Portsmouth	Norfolk Naval Shipyard	23709	804-396-3000	396-8609
Quantico	Marine Corps Base	22134	703-640-2121	640-2121
Richmond	Defense Gen. Supply Ctr	23297	804-275-3861	275-3861
Sandston	Byrd Field	23150	804-222-8884	222-8884
VirginiaB'ch	Fleet Combat Direction Systems Trng Center	23461	804-433-6234	433-6556

State/ City	Installation	ZIP Code	Information Number	Locator Number

VIRGINA (Cont.)

State/ City	Installation	ZIP Code	Information Number	Locator Number
Virginia B'ch	Fort Story	23459	804-878-1212	422-7682
Virginia B'ch	Oceana Naval Air Station	23460	804-433-2000	433-2366
Warrenton	Vint Hill Farms	22186	703-347-6000	347-6000
Williamsburg	Cheatham Annex Naval Supply Center	23185	804-887-4000	887-4000
Yorktown	CG Reserve Trng Center	23690	804-898-3500	898-3500
Yorktown	Naval Wpn Station	23691	804-887-4000	887-7661

WASHINGTON

State/ City	Installation	ZIP Code	Information Number	Locator Number
Bremerton	NS Puget Sound	98314	206-476-3466	476-3466
Oak Harbor	NAS Whidbey Island	98278	206-257-2211	257-2356
Port Angeles	CG Air Station	98362	206-457-4401	457-4401
Seattle	CG Support Center	98134	206-286-9650	286-9650
Seattle	NS Puget Sound	98115	206-526-3211	526-3237
Seattle	Fort Lawton	98199	206-281-3019	281-3030
Seattle	Seattle ANG Base	98101	206-581-1950	581-1950
Silverdale	Bangor NSB	98315	206-396-6111	396-6111
Spokane	Fairchild AFB	99011	509-247-1212	247-5875
Tacoma	Fort Lewis	98433	206-967-1110	967-6221
Tacoma	McChord AFB	98433	206-984-1910	984-2474

WEST VIRGINIA

State/ City	Installation	ZIP Code	Information Number	Locator Number
Sugar Grove	Naval Radio Stn	26815	304-249-6304	249-6304

WISCONSIN

State/ City	Installation	ZIP Code	Information Number	Locator Number
Camp D'glas	Volke Field ANG Base	54618	608-427-3341	427-3341
Milwaukee	CG Group	53207	414-291-1881	291-1881
Milwaukee	Gen. B Mitchell Field	53207	414-747-2532	747-2532
Sparta	Fort McCoy	54656	608-388-2222	388-2225

WYOMING

State/ City	Installation	ZIP Code	Information Number	Locator Number
Cheyenne	Francis E Warren AFB	82005	307-775-1110	775-1841
Guernsey	Camp Guernsey	82214	307-836-2619	836-2619

AIR FORCE, ARMY AND FLEET (NAVY AND COAST GUARD) POST OFFICES

The following list of military post office numbers shows their geographical locations. The Armed Forces World–Wide Locators provides unit locations of military members assigned overseas by their post office numbers only, by comparing these numbers to the list you can determine the overseas location of the individual military member. If you wish to obtain the unit the member is assigned, write to the locator at the APO or FPO. e.g.

Locator
APO New York 09009

APO LOCATION:
NEW YORK

09001	Reggio Calabria, Italy
09002	Mt Limbar, Sardinia, Italy
09007	Heidelberg, Germany
09008	Niederrad, Germany
09009	Ramstein AB, Germany
09011	Brunssum, Netherlands
09012	Ramstein, German
09017	Taif, Saudi Arabia
09019	Leghorn (Camp Darby), Italy
09021	Kapaun, Germany
09023	Thule AB, Greenland
09025	Schwaebish Hall, Germany
09026	Wildflecken, Germany
09028	Sandhofen, Germany
09029	Berchtesgaden, Germany
09030	Mahe, Seychelles
09031	Kitzingen, Germany
09033	Schweinfurt, Germany
09034	Baumholder, Germany
09035	Neu Ulm, Germany
09036	Wurzburg, Germany
09038	Riyadh, Saudi Arabia
09039	Frankfurt, Germany
09040	Balikisir, Turkey
09041	Riyadh, Saudi Arabia

APO LOCATION:
NEW YORK

09045	Kirchgoens, Germany
09046	Beblingen, Germany
09047	Wertheim, Germany
09048	RAF, Sculthorpe, England
09049	RAF, Greenham Common, Newbury England
09050	Bad Toelz, Germany
09051	Malatya, Turkey
09052	Zweibrucken, Germany
09053	Garmisch, Germany
09054	Kaiserslautern. Germany
09055	Chievres AB Belgium
09056	Worms, Germany
09057	Rhein-Main, Germany
09058	Worms, Germany
09059	Miesau, Germany
09060	Frankfurt, Germany
09061	Nellingen, Germany
09063	Heidelberg, Germany
09066	Erlangen, Germany
09067	Kaiserslautern,Germany
09068	Furth, Germany
09069	Bremerhaven,Germany
09070	Zirndorf, Germany
09072	Kerpen, Germany
09074	Friedberg, Germany
09075	RAF Burtonwood,England
09076	Buldingen, Germany
09077	Butzbach, Germany
09078	Muenster, Germany
09079	Frankfurt, Germany
09080	Bad Godsberg, Germany
09081	Schwetzeingen,Germany
09082	Offenbach, Germany
09083	RAF Uxbridge, Germany
09084	Kolsas, Norway
09085	Oslo, Norway
09086	Kaefertal, Germany
09088	Chievres AB,Belgium
09090	Frankfurt, Germany
09091	Gelnhausen, Germany

APO LOCATION:
NEW YORK

09092	Nurnberg, Germany
09093	Nurnberg, Germany
09094	Ramstein, Germany
09095	Germersheim, Germany
09097	Rhein-Main, Germany
09098	Bad Aibling, Germany
09099	Heidelberg, Germany
09102	Heidelberg, Germany
09103	Rhinedahlen, Germany
09104	Geilenkirchen. Germany
09105	Nurnburg, Germany
09107	Mohringen, Germany
09108	Munich, Germany
09109	Hahn, Germany
09111	Bad Kreuznach, Germany
09112	Sorghof, Germany
09114	Grafenwohr, Germany
09117	Erzurum, Turkey
09118	Izmir, Turkey
09120	RAF Wethersfield, ESS, England
09121	Sondrestrom AB, Greenland
09122	Hahn AB, Germany
09123	Spangdahlem AB, Germany
09125	RAF Fairford, England
09126	Spangdahlem AB,Germany
09127	RAF Mildenhall, Suffol,England
09128	Vaihingen, Germany
09129	RAF Feltwell, England
09130	Sembach AB, Germany
09131	Vaihingen, Germany
09132	Bitburg AB, Germany
09133	Sinop, Turkey
09136	Sembach AB, Germany
09137	Goppingen, Germany
09138	Pirmasens, Germany
09139	Bamberg, Germany
09140	Illesheim, Germany
09141	Bad Hersfeld, Germany
09142	Schwabach, Germany
09143	Giessen, Germany

APO LOCATION:
NEW YORK

09144	Fischbach, Germany
09145	Maastricht, Netherlands
09146	Fulda, Germany
09150	RAF Greenham Common, Newbury,England
09151	RAF Greenham Common, Newbury,England
09151	RAF Chicksands Aerial Mail
09152	Dhahran, Saudi Arabia
09153	Brussels City, Belgium
09154	Stuttgart, Germany
09155	Monrovia, Liberia
09159	The Hague, Netherlands
09160	Nellingen, Germany
09161	Decimomannu AB, Sardinia, Italy
09162	Aschaffenburg, Germany
09164	Karlsruhe, Germany
09165	Hanau, Germany
09166	Mannheim, Germany
09168	Vicenza, Italy
09169	Giessen, Germany
09170	Copenhagen, Denmark
09171	Muenster, Germany
09172	Oberammergau, Germany
09173	Hohenfels, Germany
09175	Darmstadt, Germany
09176	Heilbronn, Germany
09177	Ansbach, Germany
09178	Augsbach, Germany
09179	RAF Lakenheath, England
09180	Landstuhl, Germany
09182	Geibalstadt, Germany
09184	Munich, Germany
09185	Mainz, Germany
09186	Kaiserslautern, Germany
09188	Florennes AB, Belgium
09189	Pirmasens, Germany
09193	RAF,Chicksnd,Shefford,Bedford,England
09194	RAF Upper Heyford, Oxfordshire,

APO LOCATION:
NEW YORK

09198	Glouchestershire, England
09210	Menwith Hl Fl d Stn, Harrgte,Yks
09211	Darmstadt, Germany
09212	Rhein Main AB, Germany
09213	Frankfurt, Germany
09215	Hamburg, Germany
09216	Helmstedth, Germany
09220	Wiesbaden, Germany
09221	Vicenza, Italy
09222	Terminal, England
09223	Hellenikon AB, Athens, Greece
09224	Izmir, Turkey
09227	Kaiserslautern, Germany
09228	Monrovia, Liberia
09232	Ghedi AB, Italy
09236	RAF Molesworth, England
09238	RAF Alconbury, Cambrdgeshire, England
09240	Brindisi, Italy
09241	High Wycombe AS, England
09243	RAF Kemble, England
09245	Munich, Germany
09250	Katterbach, Germany
09252	Bad Kreuznach, Germany
09253	Hellenikon AB, Athens, Greece
09254	Ankara, Turkey
09279	Ludwigsburg, Germany
09281	Schwaebisch Gmund, Germany
09282	Moron AB, Spain
09283	Torrejon AB, Spain
09284	Rabat, Morocco
09285	Madrid, Spain
09286	Zaragoza AB, Spain
09289	Incirlik, Turkey
09291	Iraklion AS, Crete, Greece
09292	Soesterberg AB, Netherlands
09293	Aviano AB, Italy
09294	Pirinclik, Turkey

APO LOCATION:
NEW YORK

09298	Al-Jubail, Saudi Arabia
09305	Neubruecke, Germany
09321	Kalkar AS, Germany
09322	Idar-Oberstein, Germany
09325	Kaiserslautern, Germany
09326	Ansbach, Germany
09330	Bad Kissengen, Germany
09333	Sechkenheim, Germany
09338	Eskisekir, Turkey
09351	Ettlingen, Germany
09352	Herzogenaurauch, Germany
09353	Camp Pieri, Wiesabaden, Germany
09354	Flensberg, Germany
09355	Garlstedt, Germany
09358	Wiesbaden AB, Germany
09359	Echterdingen, Germany
09360	Knielingen, Germany
09378	RAF Croughton, Nhmptnshre, England
09380	Istanbul, Turkey
09401	Madrid, Spain
09403	Heidelberg, Germany
09405	Woodbridge, Suffolk, England
09406	Lages Fld, Terceira, Azores
09407	Munich, Germany
09411	Bindlach, Germany
09433	Verona, Italy
09451	Oberursel, Germany
09452	Amberg, Germany
09454	Goppingen, Germany
09455	Babenhausen, Germany
09457	Wiesbaden, Germany
09458	Augsburg, Germany
09607	Welford, Enlgland
09611	Berlin, Germany
09614	Islamabad, Pakistan
09615	Al Batin, Saudi Arabi
09616	Dhahran, Saudi Arabia

APO LOCATION:
NEW YORK

09633	Lindsey AS, Germany
09634	Lindsey AS, Germany
09659	Fingdales, Yorkshire, England
09662	Kinshasa, Republic of Zaire
09664	Helsinki, Finland
09666	Mainz-Kastel, Germany
09667	Brussels, Belgium
09668	Khartoum, Sudan
09669	Hessisch-Oldendorf, Germany
09670	Rimini, Italy
09671	Khamis Mushayt, Saudi Arabia
09672	Tel Aviv, Israel
09673	AFI Keflavik, Iceland
09675	Nairobi, Kenya
09677	El Gorah, Egypt
09678	Lisbon, Protugal
09679	Sharm El Shiek, Egypt
09690	Araxos, Greece
09691	Tabuk, Saudi Arabia
09692	Preum, Germany
09693	Thessaloniki, Greece
09694	Comiso, Italy
09695	Buchel AB, Germany
09696	Furth, Germany
09697	Jidda, Saudi Arabia
09701	Kitzinger, Germany
09702	Schweinfurt, Germany
09710	Offenbach, Germany
09711	Duesseldorf, Germany
09712	Rheinberg, Germany
09742	Berlin, Germany
09743	Frankfurt, Germany
09751	Crailsheim, Germany
09755	RAF Bentwaters, Suffolk, England
09757	Offenbach, Germany
09777	Paris, France
09794	Rome, Italy

APO LOCATION:
NEW YORK

09801	Wurzburg, Germany
09807	Giessen, Germany
09860	Zweibrucken AB, Germany
09862	Helsinki, Finland
09870	Karup, Denmark
09872	Zweibrucken, Germany
09892	Amman, Jordon

APO LOCATION:
MIAMI

34001	Howard AFB, Panama
34002	Albrook AFS, Panama
34003	Quarry Heights, Panama
34004	Fort Clayton, Panama
34005	Fort Wm. D. Davis, Panama
34006	Fort Kobbe, Panama
34007	Fort Amador, Panama
34008	Fort Gulick, Panama
34009	Ft. Clayton, Panama
34011	Albrook AFS, Panama
34020	San Jose, Costa Rica
34021	Managua, Nicaragua
34022	Tequcigalpa, Honduras
34023	San Salvador, El Salvador
34024	Guatemala City, Guatemala
34030	Rio de Janiero, Brazil
34031	Lima, Peru
34032	La Paz, Bolivia
34033	Santiago, Chile
34034	Bueno Aires, Argentina
34035	Monteviedo, Uraguay
34036	Asuncion, Paraguay
34037	Caracas, Venezuela
34038	Bogota, Colombia
34039	Quito, Ecuador

APO LOCATION:
MIAMI

34040	Ft Buchanan, Puerto Rico
34041	Santo Domingo, Dominican Rep
34042	Comayagua, Honduras
34061	Rodman, Panama

APO LOCATION:
SAN FRANCISCO

96208	Chunchon, Korea
96209	Sydney, Australia
96210	Misawa AB, Tokyo, Japan
96212	Taegu, Korea
96213	Taegu Aux AS, Korea
96214	Kim Hae, Korea
96218	Taegu, Korea
96220	Cheju-Do, Korea
96224	Tongduchon-ni, Korea
96230	Kadena AB, Okinawa, Japan
96231	Taejon, Korea
96235	Naha AB, Okinawa, Japan
96239	Kadena AB, Okinawa, Japan
96244	Yokota AB, Japan
96248	Makiminato, Okinawa
96251	Yong-Tae-Ri, Korea
96259	Pusan, Korea
96264	Kunsan AB, Korea
96270	Yokota AB, Japan
96271	Pyongtaek, Korea
96274	Clark AB, Manila, Philippines
96276	Kimpo AB, Korea
96277	Wallace AS, San Fernando La Union Province Philippines
96286	Clark AB, Phillipines
96287	Woomera, Australia
96292	Yokota AB, Japan

APO LOCATION:
SAN FRANCISCO

96298	John Hay AB, Baguio, Luzon, Philippines
96301	Yongsan, Korea
96302	Yongsan, Korea
96311	Clark AB, Philippines
96324	Kwanju Aux AS, Korea
96327	Andersen AFB, Guam
96328	Yokota AB, Honshu, Japan
96331	Kinzer, Okinawa, Japan
96334	Andersen AFB, Guam
96335	Camp Coiner, Yongsan, Korea
96335	Tokyo, Honshu, Japan
96343	Zama, Honshu, Japan
96344	Zukeran, Okinawa, Japan
96346	Bangkik, Thailand
96351	Andersen AFB, Guam
96356	Djakarta, Indonesia
96358	Uijongbu, Korea
96361	Yokata AB, Honshu, Japan
96366	Osan AB, Korea
96367	Kadena AB, Okinawa, Japan
96369	Alice Springs, Australia
96371	Kimpo, Korea
96397	Wongju, Kangwon-Do, Korea
96404	Canberra A.C.T., Australia
96405	Melbourne, Australia
96408	Clark AB, Philippines
96410	Clark AB, Philippines
96431	Clark AB, Philippines
96432	Clark AB, Philippines
96434	Clark AB, Philippines
96455	Osan AB, Korea
96460	Waegwan, Korea
96460	Suwon AB, Korea
96468	Bangkok, Thailand
96483	Bupyeong, Korea
96488	Bupyeong, Korea

APO LOCATION:
SAN FRANCISCO

96501	Wake Island
96503	Camp Zama, Honshu, Japan
96519	Misawa AB, Honshu, Japan
96524	Uijongbu, Korea
96528	Manila, Luzon, Philippines
96555	Kwajalein, Marshall Isand
96556	Pohakuloa, Hawaii
96570	Song Tansi, Korea
96571	Pyongtaek, Korea

APO LOCATION:
SEATTLE

98704	Clear AFS, Alaska
98713	King Salmon AFS, Alaska
98723	Galena AFS, Alaska
98733	Fort Greely, Big Delta, Alaska
98736	Shemya AFB, Alaska

FPO LOCATION:
NEW YORK

09510	London, England
09511	St. Mawgan, England
09514	Holyoch, Scotland
09515	Machrihansih, Scotland
09516	Thurso, Scotland
09518	Edzell, Scotland
09519	Brawdy, Wales
09520	Naples, Italy
09521	Naples, Italy
09522	Gaeta, Italy
09523	Sigonella, Sicily
09524	Naples, Italy
09525	Nea Makri, Greece
09526	Jafair, Bahrain

FPO LOCATION:
NEW YORK

09527	Cairo, United Arab Republic
09528	Souda Bay, Crete
09530	Nicosia, Cypress
09533	LaMaddelena Sardinia, Italy
09539	Rota, Spain
09540	Rota, Spain
09541	Cartagena, Spain
09560	Bermuda, West Indies
09571	Keflavik, Iceland
09572	Hofn, Iceland
09593	Guantanamo Bay, Cuba
09597	Argentina, Newfoundland
09598	Shelburne, Nova Scotia, Canada
34050	Punta Borinquen, Puerto Rico
34051	Roosevelt Roads, Puerto Rico
34053	Sabana Seca, Toa Ba Ja, Puerto Rico
34054	Antigua, The West Indies
34058	Andros Island, The Bahamas
34059	Ft. Amador, Panama
34060	Galetta Island, Panama
34061	Rodman, Panama

FPO LOCATION:
SEATTLE

98760	Yokohama, Japan
98761	Yokohama, Japan(Housing Area)
98762	Yokosuka, Japan(FLT ACT)
98763	Hokkaido, Japan
98764	Iwakuni, Japan
98765	Yokosuka(NAVHOSP), Japan
98766	Sasebo, Japan
98767	Atsugi, Japan
98768	Kami-Seya, Japan
98769	Chinhae, Korea
98770	Naha, (Okinawa), Japan

FPO LOCATION:
SEATTLE

98772	Futema, (Okinawa), Japan
98773	Kawasaki, (Okinawa), Japan
98777	Adak, (NAVCOMMSTA) Alaska
98778	Cmp Kuwoe (NRMC),Okinawa,Japan
98781	Iwo Jima, Bonin Islands
98782	Marcus Island, Bonin Islands
98791	Adak, Alaska
96614	Midway Islands
96630	Guam, (NAVSTA) Marianas Islands
96637	Guam, (NAS) Marianas Islands
96650	Subic Bay(FMC)(Mble Unts),Philippines
96651	Subic Bay(FMC)(Base Unts),Philippines
96652	Subic Bay(NRMC)Lzon Phlps(USNH)

FPO LOCATION:
SAN FRANCISCO

96654	Cubi Point, Luzon, Philippines
96655	Hong Kong, B.C.C.
96656	San Miguel, Philippines
96658	Tarlac, Philippines
96659	Hong Kong, B.C.C.
96680	Exmouth, Western Australia
96685	Diego Garcia Island
96690	Christchurch, New Zealand
96692	McMurdo Station, Antarctica
96699	Singapore

Navy Numbers Assigned to Mobile Forces

FPO LOCATION:
NEW YORK

09501	Navy Mobile Units, Atlantic
09502	Marine Mobile Units, Atlantic
96603	1st Marine Acft Womg. FMC
96604	3rd Force Service Support Group

96606	3rd Marine Amphibians Frcs, FMF
96607	1st Marine Brigade, FMF
09505	Ships under Military Sealift Commnd

FPO LOCATION:
SAN FRANCISCO

96601	Navy Mobile Units, Pacific
96602	Marine Mobile Units, Pacific
96605	Ships under Military Sealift Commnd

FPO LOCATION:
SEATTLE

98799	Navy Mobile Units, Pacific North

U.S. Navy and Coast Guard Fleet Post Offices

Ships Name	Hull Number	ZIP + 4 Code
USCG BASSWOOD	WLB 388	96661-3901
USCG BOUTWELL	WHEC719	98799-3902
USCG CAPE GEORGE	WPB95306	96662-3904
USCG CHASE	WHEC718	09566-3932
USCG DALLAS	WHEC716	09567-3905
USCG EAGLE	WIX 327	09568-3906
USCG ESCANABA	WMEC907	09568-3939
USCG EVERGREEN	WMEC295	09568-3936
USCG GALLATIN	WHEC721	09570-3908
USCG HAMILTON	WHEC715	09573-3931
USCG INGHAM	WHEC35	09574-3910
USCG JARVIS	WHEC725	96669-3912
USCG LANE HARRIET	WMEC903	09577-3935
USCG MALLOW	WLB 396	96672-3913
USCG MELLON	WHEC717	98799-3914
USCG MIDGETT	WHEC726	96672-3915
USCG MORGENTHAU	WHEC722	96672-3916
USCG MUNRO	WHEC724	96672-3917
USCG POLAR SEA	WAGB11	98799-3919
USCG POLAR STAR	WAGB10	98799-3920
USCG RUSH	WHEC723	96677-3921
USCG SASSFRAS	WLB 401	96678-3922
USCG SENECA	WHEC906	09587-3937

Ships Name	Hull Number	ZIP + 4 Code
USCG SHERMAN	WHEC720	96678-3923
USCG TAHOMA	WMEC908	09588-3938
USCG TAMAROA	WMEC166	09588-3933
USCG TANEY	WHEC37	09588-3925
USCG UNIMAK	WHEC379	09589-3926
USCG VIGILANT	WMEC617	09590-3934
USCG VIGOROUS	WMEC627	09590-3941
USNS ALGOL	TAKR 287	34090-4081
USNS ALTAIR	TAKR 294	34090-4080
USNS APACHE	TATF172	09564-4003
USNS ASSURANCE	AGOS 5	96660-4085
USNS AUDACIOUS	TAGO 11	96660-4042
USNS BARTLETT	AGOR 13	09565-4004
USNS BELLARTIX	TAKR 288	34090-4078
USNS BENT SILAS	TAGS 26	96661-4005
USNS CAPABLE	AGOS 16	09566-4094
USNS CAPELLA	TAKR 293	34090-4079
USNS CATAWBA	TATF 168	96662-4007
USNS CHAUVENET	TAGS 29	96662-4009
USNS COMFORT	TAH 20	09566-4008
USNS CONTENDER	AGOS 2	96662-4082
USNS DE STEIGUER	AGOR 12	96663-4012
USNS DENEBOLA	TAKR 289	09567-4019
USNS DUTTON	TAGS 22	09567-4013
USNS FURMAN	TAK 280	09569-4014
USNS HARKNESS	TAGS 32	09573-4015
USNS HASSAYAMPA	TAO 145	96667-4016
USNS HESS H H	TAGS 38	96667-4018
USNS HIGGINS ANDREW	TAO 190	96667-4001
USNS INDOMITABLE	AGOS 7	96668-4067
USNS INVINCIBLE	TAGO 10	09574-4041
USNS KAISER HENRY J	TAO 187	09576-4086
USNS KANE	TAGS 27	09576-4021
USNS KAWISHIWI	TAO 146	96670-4022
USNS KILAUEA	TAE 26	96670-4023
USNS LENTHALL JOHN	TAO 189	09577-4091
USNS LYNCH	AGOR 7	09577-4025
USNS MARSHFIELD	TAK 282	34092-4026
USNS MAURY	TAGS 39	09578-4029
USNS MERCURY	TAJR 10	96672-4028
USNS MERCY	TAH 19	96672-4090
USNS MISPILLION	TAO 105	96672-4030
USNS MISSISSINEWA	TAO 144	34092-4031
USNS MIZAR	AGOR 11	09578-4032
USNS MOHAWK	TATF 170	09578-4033
USNS MYER ALBERT J	TARC 6	96672-4034
USNS NARRAGANSETT	TATF 167	96673-4035
USNS NAVAJO	TATF 169	96673-4036
USNS NAVASOTA	TAO 106	96673-4037
USNS NEOSHO	TAO 143	09579-4039

Ships Name	Hull Number	ZIP + 4 Code
USNS NEPTUNE	TARC 2	09579-4040
USNS OBSERVATION IS	TAGM 23	96674-4043
USNS PASSUMPSIC	TAO 107	96675-4044
USNS PAWCATUCK	TAO 108	09582-4054
USNS PERSISTENT	AGOS 6	09582-4047
USNS POINT LOMA	TAGD 2	96675-4000
USNS POLLUX	TAKR 290	34092-4062
USNS PONCHATOULA	TAO 148	96675-4046
USNS POWHATAN	TATF 166	09582-4048
USNS PREVAIL	AGOS 8	09582-4002
USNS RANGE SENTINEL	TAGM 22	34092-4049
USNS REDSTONE	TAGM 20	34092-4050
USNS REGULUS	TAKR 292	96677-4010
USNS RIGEL	TAF 58	09586-4051
USNS SEALIFT ANTARC	TAOT 176	09587-4053
USNS SEALIFT ARABIA	TAOT 169	09587-4054
USNS SEALIFT ARCTIC	TAOT 175	09587-4055
USNS SEALIFT ATLANT	TAOT 172	09587-4056
USNS SEALIFT CARIBB	TAOT 174	09587-4057
USNS CHINA SEA	TAOT 170	09587-4058
USNS INDIAN OCEAN	TAOT 171	09587-4059
USNS MEDITERRANEAN	TAOT 173	09587-4060
USNS SEALIFT PACIFIC	TAOT 168	09587-4061
USNS SIOUX	TATF 171	96678-4063
USNS SIRIUS	TAFS 8	09587-4064
USNS SPICA	TAFS 9	96678-4066
USNS STALWART	TGOS 1	09587-4077
USNS TITAN	AGOS 15	96679-4093
USNS TRIUMPH	AGOS 4	96679-4093
USNS TRUCKEE	TAO 147	09588-4068
USNS VANGUARD	TAG 194	34093-4069
USNS VEGA	TAK 286	34093-4070
USNS VINDICATOR	AGOS 3	09590-4083
USNS WACCAMAW	TAO 109	34093-4072
USNS WALTERS S DIEH	TAO 193	96663-4020
USNS WILKES	TAGS 33	09591-4073
USNS WORTHY	AGOS 14	09591-4092
USNS WYMAN	TAGS 34	96683-4074
USNS ZEUS	TARC 7	96687-4076
USS ACADIA	AD 42	96647-2530
USS ADAMS CHARLES F	DDG 2	34090-1232
USS ADAMS JOHN	SSBN 620	34093-2009
USS ADAMS JOHN (B)	SSBN 620	34093-2010
USS ADAMS JOHN (G)	SSBN 620	34093-2011
USS ADROIT	MSO 509	09564-1919
USS AFFRAY	MSO 511	09564-1920
USS AINSWORTH	FF 1090	09564-1450
USS ALABAMA	SSBN 731	98799-2108
USS ALABAMA (B)	SSBN 731	98799-2109
USS ALABAMA (G)	SSBN 731	98799-2110

Ships Name	Hull Number	ZIP + 4 Code
USS ALAMO	LSD 33	96660-1721
USS ALASKA	SSBN 732	98799-2111
USS ALASKA (B)	SSBN 732	98799-2112
USS ALASKA (G)	SSBN 732	98799-2113
USS ALBUQUERQUE	SSN 706	09564-2386
USS AMERICA	CV 66	09531-2790
USS ANCHORAGE	SD 36	96660-1724
USS ANTIETAM	CG 54	96660-1174
USS ANTRIM	FFG 20	34090-1476
USS AQUILA	PHM 4	34090-3411
USS ARCHERFISH	SSN 678	98799-2358
USS ARIES	PHM 5	34090-3412
USS ARKANSAS	CGN 41	96660-1168
USS ASPRO	SSN 648	96660-2334
USS ATLANTA	SSN 712	09564-2392
USS AUGUSTA	SSN 710	09564-2390
USS AUSTIN	LPD 4	09564-1707
USS AVENGER	CM 1	34090-1921
USS AYLWIN	FF 1081	09564-1441
USS BADGER	FF 1071	96661-1431
USS BAGLEY	FF 1069	96661-1429
USS BAINBRIDGE	CGN 25	09565-1161
USS BALTIMORE	SSN 704	09565-2384
USS BANCROFT GEORGE	SSBN 643	34090-2066
USS BANCROFT GEORGE (B)	SSBN 643	34090-2067
USS BANCROFT GEORGE (G)	SSBN 643	34090-2068
USS BARB	SSN 596	96661-2312
USS BARBEL	SS 580	96661-3402
USS BARBEY	FF 1088	96661-1448
USS BARBOUR COUNTY	LST 1195	96661-1816
USS BARNEY	DDG 6	09565-1236
USS BARNSTABLE COUN	LST 1197	09565-1818
USS BATES WILLIAM H	SSN 680	98799-2360
USS BATFISH	SSN 681	34090-2361
USS BATON ROUGE	SSN 689	09565-2369
USS BEARY DONALD B	FF 1085	09565-1445
USS BEAUFORT	ATS 2	96661-3218
USS BELKNAP	CG 26	09565-1149
USS BELLEAU WOOD	LHA 3	96623-1610
USS BERGALL	SSN 667	09565-2347
USS BERKELEY	DDG 15	96661-1245
USS BIDDLE	CG 34	09565-1157
USS BILLFISH	SSN 676	09565-2356
USS BIRMINGHAM	SSN 695	96661-2375
USS BLAKELY	FF 1072	34090-1432
USS BLUE RIDGE	LCC 19	96628-3300
USS BLUEBACK	SS 581	96661-3403
USS BLUEFISH	SSN 675	09565-2355
USS BOLIVAR SIMON	SSBN 641	34090-2060
USS BOLIVAR SIMON (B)	SSBN 641	34090-2061

Ships Name	Hull Number	ZIP + 4 Code
USS BOLIVAR SIMON (G)	SSBN 641	34090-2062
USS BOLSTER	ARS 38	96661-3201
USS BONEFISH	SS 582	34090-3404
USS BOONE	FFG 28	34093-1484
USS BOONE DANIEL	SSBN 629	34090-2033
USS BOONE DANIEL (B)	SSBN 629	34090-2034
USS BOONE DANIEL (G)	SSBN 629	34090-2035
USS BOSTON	SSN 703	09565-2383
USS BOULDER	LST 1190	09565-1811
USS BOWEN	FF 1079	09565-1439
USS BREMERTO	SSN 698	96661-2378
USS BREWTON	FF 1086	96661-1446
USS BRISCOE	DD 977	09565-1215
USS BRISTOL COUNTY	LST 1198	96661-1819
USS BRONSTEIN	FF 1037	96661-1400
USS BROWN JESSE L	FF 1089	34090-1449
USS BRUNSWICK	ATS 3	96661-3219
USS BUCHANAN	DDG 14	96661-1244
USS BUFFALO	SSN 715	96661-2395
USS BUNKER HILL	CG 52	96661-1172
USS BUTTE	AE 27	09565-3005
USS BYRD RICHARD E	DDG 23	09565-1253
USS CABLE FRANK	AS 40	34086-2615
USS CALHOUN JOHN C	SSBN 630	34090-2036
USS CALHOUN JOHN C (B)	SSBN 630	34090-2037
USS CALHOUN JOHN C (G)	SSBN 630	34090-2038
USS CALIFORNIA	CGN 36	96662-1163
USS CALLAGHAN	DDG 994	96662-1266
USS CALOOSAHATCHEE	AO 98	09566-3016
USS CAMDEN	AOE 2	98799-3013
USS CANISTEO	AO 99	09566-3017
USS CANOPUS	AS 34	34087-2595
USS CAPE COD	AD 43	96649-2535
USS CAPODANNO	FF 1093	09566-1453
USS CARON	DD 970	09566-1208
USS CARR	FFG 52	34090-1506
USS CARVER GEORGE W	SSBN 656	09566-2081
USS CARVER GEORGE W (B)	SSBN 656	09566-2082
USS CARVER GEORGE W (G)	SSBN 656	09566-2083
USS CAVALLA	SSN 684	96662-2364
USS CAYUGA	LST 1186	96662-1807
USS CHANDLER	DDG 996	96662-1268
USS CHARLESTON	LKA 113	09566-1700
USS CHICAGO	SSN 721	96662-2401
USS CIMARRON	AO 177	96662-3018
USS CINCINNATI	SSN 693	09566-2373
USS CITY OF CORPUS	SSN 705	09566-2385
USS CLARK	FFG 11	09566-1469
USS CLAY HENRY	SSBN 625	34090-2021
USS CLAY HENRY (B)	SSBN 625	34090-2022

Ships Name	Hull Number		ZIP + 4 Code
USS CLAY HENRY (G)	SSBN	625	34090-2023
USS CLEVELAND	LPD	7	96662-1710
USS COCHRANE	DDG	21	96662-1251
USS COMPTE DE GRASS	DD	974	09566-1212
USS CONCORD	AFS	5	09566-3034
USS CONNOLE	FF	1056	09566-1416
USS CONOLLY	DD	979	09566-1217
USS CONQUEST	MSO	488	98799-1915
USS CONSERVER	ARS	39	96662-3202
USS CONSTANT	MSO	427	96662-1900
USS CONSTELLATION	CV	64	96635-2780
USS CONYNGHAM	DDG	17	09566-1247
USS COOK	FF	1083	96662-1443
USS COONTZ	DDG	40	09566-1258
USS COPELAND	FFG	25	96662-1481
USS CORAL SEA	CV	43	09550-2720
USS CORONADO	AGF	11	96662-3330
USS CROMMELIN	FFG	37	96662-1492
USS CURTS	FFG	38	96662-1493
USS CUSHING	DD	985	96662-1223
USS DACE	SSN	607	98799-2320
USS DAHLGREN	DDG	43	09567-1261
USS DALE	CG	19	34090-1143
USS DALLAS	SSN	700	09567-2380
USS DANIELS JOSEPHUS	CG	27	09567-1150
USS DARTER	SS	576	96663-3401
USS DAVID ALBERT	FF	1050	96663-1410
USS DAVIS RODNEY M	FFG	60	96663-1514
USS DE WERT	FFG	45	34090-1499
USS DEFENDER	MCM	2	09567-1922
USS DENVER	LPD	9	96663-1712
USS DETROIT	AOE	4	09567-3015
USS DEWEY	DDG	45	34090-1263
USS DEYO	DD	989	34090-1227
USS DIXON	AS	37	96648-2605
USS DOLPHIN	AGSS	555	96663-1430
USS DOWNES	FF	1070	96663-3400
USS DOYLE	FFG	39	34090-1494
USS DRUM	SSN	677	96663-2357
USS DUBUQUE	LPD	8	96663-1711
USS DULUTH	LPD	6	96663-1709
USS DUNCAN	FFG	10	96663-1468
USS DURHAM	LKA	114	96663-1701
USS EDENTON	ATS	1	09568-3217
USS EISENHOWER DWIGHT	CVN	69	09532-2830
USS EL PASO	LKA	117	09568-1704
USS ELLIOT	DD	967	96664-1205
USS ELROD	FFG	55	34091-1509
USS ENGAGE	MSO	433	34091-1901
USS ENGLAND	CG	22	96664-1146

Ships Name	Hull Number		ZIP + 4 Code
USS ENHANCE	MSO	437	98799-1902
USS ENTERPRISE	CVN	65	96636-2810
USS ESTEEM	MSO	438	98799-1902
USS ESTOCIN	FFG	15	09569-1473
USS EXCEL	MSO	439	96664-1904
USS EXPLOIT	MSO	440	09568-1905
USS EXULTANT	MSO	441	34091-1906
USS FAIRFAX COUNTY	LST	1193	09569-1814
USS FANNING	FF	1076	96665-1436
USS FARRAGUT	DDG	37	09569-1255
USS FEARLESS	MSO	442	34091-1907
USS FIFE	DD	991	96665-1229
USS FINBACK	SSN	670	09569-2350
USS FITCH AUBREY	FFG	34	34091-1490
USS FLASHER	SSN	613	96665-2324
USS FLETCHER	DD	992	96665-1230
USS FLINT	AE	32	96665-3008
USS FLORIDA	SSBN	728	98799-2099
USS FLORIDA (B)	SSBN	728	98799-2100
USS FLORIDA (G)	SSBN	728	98799-2101
USS FLORIKAN	ASR	9	96665-3207
USS FLYING FISH	SSN	673	09569-2353
USS FORD	FFG	54	96665-1508
USS FORRESTAL	CV	59	34080-2730
USS FORT FISHER	LSD	40	96665-1728
USS FORT McHENRY	LSD	43	96665-1731
USS FORTIFY	MSO	446	09569-1909
USS FOSTER PAUL F	DD	964	96665-1202
USS FOX	CG	33	96665-1156
USS FRANKLIN BENJAMIN	SSBN	640	34091-2057
USS FRANKLIN BENJAMIN (B)	SSBN	640	34091-2058
USS FRANKLIN BENJAMIN (G)	SSBN	640	34091-2059
USS FREDERICK	LST	1184	96665-1805
USS FRESNO	LST	1182	96665-1803
USS FULTON	AS	11	09534-2565
USS GALLANT	MSO	489	96666-1916
USS GALLERY	FFG	26	34091-1482
USS GARY	FFG	51	96666-1505
USS GATES THOMAS S	CG	51	09570-1171
USS GATO	SSN	615	09570-2326
USS GEMINI	PHM	6	34091-3413
USS GEORGIA	SSBN	729	98799-2102
USS GEORGIA (B)	SSBN	729	98799-2103
USS GEORGIA (G)	SSBN	729	98799-2104
USS GERMANTOWN	LSD	42	96666-1730
USS GLOVER	FF	1098	09570-1458
USS GOLDSBOROUGH	DDG	20	96666-1250
USS GOMPERS SAMUEL	AD	37	96641-2515
USS GRANT ULYSSES S	SSBN	631	09570-2039
USS GRANT ULYSSES (B)	SSBN	631	09570-2040

Ships Name	Hull Number		ZIP + 4 Code
USS GRANT ULYSSES (G)	SSBN	631	09570-2041
USS GRAPPLE	ARS	53	09570-3223
USS GRASP	ARS	51	09570-3220
USS GRAY	FF	1054	96666-1414
USS GRAYLING	SSN	646	34091-2332
USS GREENLING	SSN	614	09570-2325
USS GRIDLEY	CG	21	96666-1145
USS GROTON	SSN	694	09570-2374
USS GROVES STEPHEN	FFG	29	34091-1485
USS GUADALCANAL	LPH	7	09562-1635
USS GUAM	LPH	9	09563-1640
USS GUARDFISH	SSN	612	96666-2323
USS GUITARRO	SSN	665	96666-2345
USS GUNSTON HALL	LSD	44	09573-1732
USS GURNARD	SSN	662	96666-2342
USS HADDO	SSN	604	96667-2317
USS HADDOCK	SSN	621	96667-2328
USS HALEAKALA	AE	25	96667-3004
USS HALL JOHN L	FFG	32	34091-1488
USS HALSEY	CG	23	96667-1147
USS HALYBURTON	FFG	40	34091-1495
USS HAMILTON ALEXAN	SSBN	617	09573-2003
USS HAMILTON ALEX (B)	SSBN	617	09573-2004
USS HAMILTON ALEX (G)	SSBN	617	09573-2005
USS HAMMERHEAD	SSN	663	09573-2343
USS HAMMOND FRANCIS	FF	1067	96667-1427
USS HANCOCK JOHN	DD	981	34091-1219
USS HARLAN COUNTY	LST	1196	09573-1817
USS HART THOMAS C	FF	1092	09573-1452
USS HAWES	FFG	53	34091-1507
USS HAWKBILL	SSN	666	96667-2346
USS HAYLER	DD	997	09573-1231
USS HELENA	SSN	725	96667-2405
USS HEPBURN	FF	1055	96667-1415
USS HERCULES	PHM	2	34091-3409
USS HERMITAGE	LSD	34	09573-1722
USS HEWES JOSEPH	FF	1078	34091-1438
USS HEWITT	DD	966	96667-1204
USS HILL HARRY W	DD	986	96667-1224
USS HOEL	DDG	13	96667-1243
USS HOIST	ARS	40	09573-3203
USS HOLLAND	AS	32	34079-2585
USS HOLT HAROLD E	FF	1074	96667-1434
USS HONOLULU	SSN	718	96667-2398
USS HORNE	CG	30	96667-1153
USS HOUSTON	SSN	713	96667-2393
USS HOUSTON SAM	SSN	609	96667-2321
USS HUNLEY	AS	31	09559-2580
USS ILLUSIVE	MSO	448	34091-1910
USS IMPERVIOUS	MSO	449	34091-1911

Ships Name	Hull Number	ZIP + 4 Code
USS IMPLICIT	MSO 455	98799-1912
USS INCHON	LPH 12	09529-1655
USS INDEPENDENCE	CV 62	96618-2760
USS INDIANAPOLIS	SSN 697	96668-2377
USS INFLICT	MSO 456	09574-1913
USS INGERSOLL	DD 990	96668-1228
USS IOWA	BB 61	09546-1100
USS IWO JIMA	LPH 2	09561-1625
USS JACK	SSN 605	09575-2318
USS JACKSON ANDREW	SSBN 619	09575-2006
USS JACKSON ANDRE (B)	SSBN 619	09575-2007
USS JACKSON ANDRE (G)	SSBN 619	09575-2008
USS JACKSON HENRY M	SSBN 730	98799-2105
USS JACKSON HENRY (B)	SSBN 730	98799-2106
USS JACKSON HENRY (G)	SSBN 730	98799-2107
USS JACKSON STONEWA	SSBN 634	34091-2048
USS JACKSON STONE (B)	SSBN 634	34091-2049
USS JACKSON STONE (G)	SSBN 634	34091-2050
USS JACKSONVILLE	SSN 699	09575-2379
USS JAMES RUEBEN	FFG 57	96669-1511
USS JARRETT	FFG 33	96669-1489
USS JASON	AR 8	96644-2560
USS JOUETT	CG 29	96669-1152
USS JUNEAU	LPD 10	96669-1713
USS KALAMAZOO	AOR 6	09576-3028
USS KAMEHAMEHA	SSBN 642	09576-2063
USS KAMEHAMEHA	SSBN 642	09576-2064
USS KAMEHAMEHA	SSBN 642	09576-2065
USS KANSAS CITY	AOR 3	96670-3025
USS KAUFFMAN	FFG 59	09576-1513
USS KENNEDY JOHN F	CV 67	09538-2800
USS KEY FRANCIS SCO	SSBN 657	34091-2084
USS KEY FRANCIS S (B)	SSBN 657	34091-2085
USS KEY FRANCIS S (G)	SSBN 657	34091-2086
USS KEY WEST	SSN 722	09576-2402
USS KIDD	DDG 993	09576-1265
USS KING	DDG 41	09576-1259
USS KING JOHN	DDG 3	09595-1233
USS KINKAID	DD 965	96670-1203
USS KIRK	FF 1087	96670-1447
USS KISKA	AE 35	96670-3011
USS KITTIWAKE	ASR 13	09576-3208
USS KITTY HAWK	CV 63	09535-2770
USS KLAKRING	FFG 42	34091-1497
USS KNOX	FF 1052	96670-1412
USS LA JOLLA	SSN 701	96671-2381
USS LA MOURE COUNT	LST 1194	09577-1815
USS LAFAYETTE	SSBN 616	09577-2000
USS LAFAYETTE (B)	SSBN 616	09577-2001
USS LAFAYETTE (G)	SSBN 616	09577-2002

Ships Name	Hull Number		ZIP + 4 Code
USS LAKE CHAMPLAIN	CG	57	96671-1177
USS LAND EMORY S	AS	39	09545-2610
USS LANG	FF	1060	96671-1420
USS LAPON	SSN	661	09577-2341
USS LASALLE	AFG	3	09577-3320
USS LAWRENCE	DDG	4	09577-1234
USS LEADER	MSO	490	34091-1917
USS LEAHY	CG	16	96671-1140
USS LEFTWICH	DD	984	96671-1222
USS LEWIS & CLARK	SBN	644	34091-2069
USS LEWIS & CLARK (B)	SBN	644	34091-2070
USS LEWIS & CLARK (G)	SBN	644	34091-2071
USS LEXINGTON	AVT	16	34088-2700
USS LEYTE GULF	CG	55	34091-1175
USS LIPSCOMB GLENAR	SSN	685	09577-2365
USS LOCKWOOD	FF	1064	96671-1424
USS LONG BEACH	CGN	9	96671-1160
USS LOS ANGELES	SSN	688	96671-2368
USS LOUISVILLE	SSN	724	96671-2404
USS LUCE	DDG	38	34091-1256
USS MACDONOUGH	DDG	39	34092-1257
USS MADISON JAMES	SSBN	627	34092-2027
USS MADISON JAMES (B)	SSBN	627	34092-2028
USS MADISON JAMES (G)	SSBN	627	34092-2029
USS MAHAN	DDG	42	34092-1260
USS MANITOWOC	LST	1180	09578-1801
USS MARS	AFS1	1	96672-3030
USS MARSHALL GEORGE	SSBN	654	09578-2075
USS MARSHALL GEORGE (B)	SSBN	654	09578-2076
USS MARSHALL GEORGE (G)	SSBN	654	09578-2077
USS MARSHALL JOHN	SSN	611	09578-2322
USS MAUNA KEA	AE	22	96672-3001
USS MCCANDLESS	FF	1084	09578-1444
USS MCCLOY	FF	1038	09578-1401
USS MCCLUSKY	FFG	41	96672-1496
USS MCCORMICK LYNDE	DDG	8	96672-1238
USS MCINERNEY	FFG	8	34092-1466
USS MCKEE	AS	41	96621-2620
USS MEMPHIS	SSN	691	09578-2371
USS MERRILL	DD	976	96672-1214
USS MERRIMACK	AO	179	09578-3020
USS MEYERKORD	FF	1058	96672-1418
USS MICHIGAN	SSBN	727	98799-2096
USS MICHIGAN(B)	SSBN	727	98799-2097
USS MICHIGAN(G)	SSBN	727	98799-2098
USS MIDWAY	CV	41	96631-2710
USS MILLER	FF	1091	09578-1451
USS MILWAUKEE	AOR	2	09578-3024
USS MINNEAPOL ST PA	SSN	708	09578-2388
USS MISSISSIPPI	CGN	40	09578-1167

Ships Name	Hull Number		ZIP + 4 Code
USS MISSOURI	BB	63	96689-1120
USS MOBILE	LKA	115	96672-1702
USS MOBILE BAY	CG	53	34092-1173
USS MOINESTER	FF	1097	09578-1457
USS MOHONGAHELA	AO	178	09578-3019
USS MONROE JAMES	SSBN	622	34092-2012
USS MONROE JAMES(B)	SSBN	622	34092-2013
USS MONROE JAMES(G)	SSBN	622	34092-2014
USS MONTGOMERY ELM	FF	1082	34092-1442
USS MOOSBRUGGER	DD	980	34092-1218
USS MORISON SM ELIO	FFG	13	34092-1471
USS MOUNT BAKER	AE	34	34092-3010
USS MOUNT HOOD	AE	29	96672-3007
USS MOUNT VERNON	LSD	39	96672-1727
USS MOUNT WHITNEY	LCC	20	09517-3310
USS NARWHAL	SSN	671	34092-2351
USS NASHVILLE	LPD	13	09579-1715
USS NASSAU	LHA	4	09557-1615
USS NEVADA	SSBN	733	98799-2114
USS NEVADA (B)	SSBN	733	98799-2115
USS NEVADA (G)	SSBN	733	98799-2116
USS NEW JERSEY	BB	62	96688-1110
USS NEW ORLEANS	LPH	11	96627-1650
USS NEW YORK CITY	SSN	696	96673-2376
USS NEWPORT	LST	1179	09579-1800
USS NEWPORT NEWS	SSN	750	095792406
USS NIAGARA FALLS	AFS	3	96673-3032
USS NICHOLAS	FFG	47	34092-1501
USS NICHOLSON	DD	982	34092-1220
USS NIMITZ	CVN	68	98780-2820
USS NITRO	AE	23	09579-3002
USS NORFOLK	SSN	714	09579-2394
USS O'BANNON	DD	987	34092-1225
USS O'BRIEN	DD	975	96674-1213
USS OGDEN	LPD	5	96674-1708
USS OHIO	SSBN	726	98799-2093
USS OHIO (B)	SSBN	726	98799-2094
USS OHIO (G)	SSBN	726	98799-2095
USS OKINAWA	LPH	3	96625-1630
USS OLDENDORF	DD	972	96674-1210
USS OLYMPIA	SSN	717	96674-2397
USS OMAHA	SSN	692	96674-2372
USS OPPORTUNE	ARS	41	09581-3204
USS ORION	AS	18	09513-2570
USS ORTOLAN	ASR	22	34092-3212
USS OUELLET	FF	1077	96674-1437
USS PAIUTE	ATF	159	09682-3215
USS PAPAGO	ATF	160	09582-3215
USS PARCHE	SSN	683	96675-7363
USS PARGO	SSN	650	09582-2336

Ships Name	Hull Number		ZIP + 4 Code
USS PATTERSON	FF	1061	09582-1421
USS PAUL	FF	1080	34092-1440
USS PEARY ROBERY E	FF	1073	95675-1443
USS PEGASUS	PHM	1	34092-3408
USS PELELIU	LHA	5	96624-1620
USS PENSACOLA	LSD	38	09582-1726
USS PEORIA	LST	1183	96675-1804
USS PERMIT	SSN	594	96675-2310
USS PERRY OLIVER H	FFG	7	09582-1465
USS PETERSON	DD	969	09582-1207
USS PETREL	ASR	14	34092-3209
USS PHARRIS	FF	1094	09582-1454
USS PHILADELPHIA	SSN	690	09582-2370
USS PHILIP GEORGE	FFG	12	96675-1470
USS PHILIPPINE SEA	CG	58	34093-1178
USS PHOENIX	SSN	702	09582-2382
USS PIGEON	ASR	21	96675-3211
USS PINTADO	SSN	672	96675-2352
USS PITTSBURG	SSN	720	09582-2400
USS PLATTE	AO	186	09582-3022
USS PLUCK	MSO	464	96675-1914
USS PLUNGER	SSN	595	96675-2311
USS POGY	SSN	647	96675-2333
USS POLK JAMES K	SSBN	645	09582-2072
USS POLK JAMES K (B)	SSBN	645	09582-2073
USS POLK JAMES K (G)	SSBN	645	09582-2074
USS POLLACK	SSN	603	96675-2316
USS PONCE	LPD	15	09582-1717
USS PORTLAND	LSD	37	09582-1725
USS PROTSMOUTH	SSN	707	96675-2387
USS PRAIRIE	AD	15	96639-2500
USS PRATT WILLIAM	DDG	44	34092-1262
USS PREBLE	DDG	46	09582-1264
USS PRESERVER	ARS	8	09582-3200
USS PROTEUS	AS	19	96646-2575
USS PROVIDENCE	SSN	719	09582-2399
USS PUFFER	SSN	652	96675-2338
USS PUGET SOUND	AD	38	09544-2520
USS PULASKI CASIMI	SSBN	633	34092-2045
USS PULASKI CASI (B)	SSBN	633	34092-2046
USS PULASKI CASI (G)	SSBN	633	34092-2047
USS PULLER LEWIS	FFG	23	96675-1479
USS PYRO	AE	24	96675-3003
USS QUEENFISH	SSN	651	96676-2337
USS RACINE	LST	1191	96677-1812
USS RADFORD ARTH	DD	968	09586-1206
USS RALEIGH	LPD	1	09586-1705
USS RANGER	CV	61	96633-2750
USS RATHBURNE	FF	1057	96677-1417
USS RAY	SSN	653	34092-2339

Ships Name	Hull Number	ZIP + 4 Code
USS RAY DAVID R	DD 971	96677-1209
USS RAYBURN SAM	SSBN 635	34092-2051
USS RAYBURN SAM(B)	SSBN 635	34092-2052
USS RAYBURN SAM(G)	SSBN 635	34092-2053
USS REASONER	FF 1063	96677-1423
USS RECLAIMER	ARS 42	96677-3205
USS RECOVERY	ARS 43	09586-3206
USS REEVES	CG 24	96677-1148
USS REID	FFG 30	96677-1486
USS RENTZ	FFG 46	96677-1500
USS RICKETTS CLUADE	DDG 5	09586-1235
USS RICKOVER HYMAN	SSN 709	09586-2389
USS RIVERS L MENDEL	SSN 686	34092-2366
USS ROANOKE	AOR 7	96677-3029
USS ROARK	FF 1053	96677-1242
USS ROBERTS SAMUEL	FFG 58	09586-1512
USS ROBISON	DDG 12	96677-1242
USS RODGERS JOHN	DD 983	34092-1221
USS ROGERS WILL	SSBN 659	09586-2090
USS ROGERS WILL(B)	SSBN 659	09586-2091
USS ROGERS WILL(G)	SSBN 659	09586-2092
USS ROOSEVELT THEO	CVN 71	09599-2871
USS RUSSEL RICHARD	SSN 687	96677-2367
USS SACRAMENTO	AOE 1	96678-3012
USS SAFEGUARD	ARS 50	96678-3221
USS SAGINAW	LST 1188	09587-1809
USS SAINT LOUIS	LKA 116	96678-1703
USS SAIPAN	LHA 2	09549-1605
USS SALT LAKE CITY	SSN 716	96678-2396
USS SALVOR	ARS 52	96678-3222
USS SAMPSON	DDG 10	34093-1240
USS SAN BERNARDINO	LST 1189	96678-1810
USS SAN DIEGO	AFS 6	09587-3035
USS SAN FRANSISCO	SSN 711	96678-1810
USS SAN JACINTO	CG 56	09587-1176
USS SAN JOSE	AFS 7	96678-3036
USS SAND LANCE	SSN 660	09587-2340
USS SANTA BARBERA	AE 28	34093-3006
USS SARATOGA	CV 60	34078-2740
USS SARGO	SSN 583	96678-2303
USS SAVANNAH	AOR 4	09587-3026
USS SCHENECTADY	LST 1185	96678-1806
USS SCOTT	DDG 995	09587-1267
USS SCULPIN	SSN 590	09587-2307
USS SEA DEVIL	SSN 664	34093-2344
USS SEAHORSE	SSN 669	98799-2349
USS SEATTLE	AOE 3	09587-3014
USS SELLERS	DDG 11	34093-1241
USS SEMMES	DDG 591	34093-1248
USS SHARK	SSN 591	09587-2308

Ships Name	Hull Number		ZIP + 4 Code
USS SHASTA	AE	33	96678-3009
USS SHENANDOAH	AD	44	09551-2540
USS SHIELDS MARVIN	FF	1066	96678-1426
USS SHREVEPORT	LPD	12	09587-1714
USS SIERRA	AD	18	34084-2505
USS SILVERSIDES	SSN	679	09587-2359
USS SIMON LAKE	AS	33	09536-2590
USS SIMPSON	FFG	56	09587-1510
USS SIMS W S	FF	1059	34093-1419
USS SKIPJACK	SSN	585	09587-2305
USS SOUTH CAROLINA	CGN	37	09587-1164
USS SPADEFISH	SSN	668	09587-2348
USS SPARTANBURG CO	LST	1192	09587-1813
USS SPEAR	AS	36	09547-2600
USS SPEIGEL GROVE	LSD	32	09587-1720
USS SPRAGUE CLIFTON	FFG	16	09587-1474
USS SPRUANCE	DD	963	34093-1201
USS STANDLEY WILL	CG	32	96678-1155
USS STARK	FFG	31	34093-1487
USS STEIN	FF	1065	96678-1425
USS STERETT	CG	31	96678-1154
USS STIMSON HENRY L	SSBN	655	34093-2078
USS STIMSON HENRY (B)	SSBN	655	34093-2079
USS STIMSON HENRY (G)	SSBN	655	34093-2080
USS STODDERT BENJAM	DDG	22	96678-1252
USS SRTAUSS JOSEPH	DDG	16	96678-1246
USS STUMP	DD	978	09587-1216
USS STURGEON	SSN	637	34093-2329
USS SUBMARINE NR1	NR	1	09587-3405
USS SUMTER	LST	1181	09587-3031
USS SUNBIRD	ASR	15	09587-3210
USS SUNFISH	SSN	649	34093-2335
USS SURIBACHI	AE	21	09587-3000
USS STYLVANIA	AFS	2	09587-3031
USS TARAWA	LHA	1	96622-1600
USS TATTNALL	DDG	19	34093-1249
USS TAURUS	PHM	3	34093-3410
USS TAUTOG	SSN	639	96679-2331
USS TAYLOR	FFG	50	34093-1504
USS TECUMSEH	SSBN	628	34093-2030
USS TECUMSEH(B)	SSBN	628	34093-2031
USS TECUMSEH(G)	SSBN	628	34093-2032
USS TENNESSEE	SSBN	734	34093-2117
USS TEXAS	CGN	39	96679-1166
USS THACH	FFG	43	96679-1498
USS THORN	DD	988	34093-1226
USS TICONDEROGA	CG	47	09588-1158
USS TINOSA	SSN	606	09588-2319
USS TISDALE MAHLON	FFG	27	96679-1483
USS TOWERS	DDG	9	96679-1239

Ships Name	Hull Number		ZIP + 4 Code
USS TRENTON	LPD	14	09588-1716
USS TREPANG	SSN	674	09588-2354
USS TRIPOLI	LPH	10	96626-1645
USS TRIPPE	FF	1075	09588-1435
USS TRUETTE	FF	1095	09588-1455
USS TRUXTUN	CGN	35	96679-1162
USS TULIBEE	SSN	597	09588-2313
USS TUNNY	SSN	682	98799-2362
USS TURNER RICHMOND	CG	20	34093-1144
USS TUSCALOOSA	LST	1187	96679-1808
USS UNDREWOOD	FFG	36	34093-1491
USS VALDEZ	FF	1096	09590-1456
USS VALLEJO MARIANO	SSBN	658	34093-2087
USS VALLEJO MARIA (B)	SSBN	658	34093-2088
USS VALLEJO MARIA (G)	SSBN	658	34093-2089
USS VALLEY FORGE	CG	50	96682-1169
USS VANCOUVER	LPD	2	96682-1706
USS VANDERGRIFT	FFG	48	96682-1502
USS VINCENNES	CG	49	96682-1169
USS VINSON CARL	CVN	70	96629-2840
USS VIRGINIA	CGN	38	09590-1165
USS VOGE	FF	1047	34093-1407
USS VON STEUBEN	SSBN	632	34093-2042
USS VON STEUBEN (B)	SSBN	632	34093-2043
USS VON STEUBEN (G)	SSBN	632	34093-2044
USS VREELAND	FF	1068	09590-1428
USS VULCAN	AR	5	09548-2545
USS WABASH	AOR	5	96683-3027
USS WADDELL	DDG	24	96683-1254
USS WADSWORTH	FFG	9	96683-1467
USS WAINWRIGHT	CG	28	34093-1151
USS WEBSTER DANIEL	SSBN	626	09591-2024
USS WEBSTER DANIEL (B)	SSBN	626	09591-2025
USS WEBSTER DANIEL (G)	SSBN	626	09591-2026
USS WHALE	SSN	638	09591-2330
USS WHIDBEY ISLAND	LSD	41	09591-1729
USS WHIPPLE	FF	1062	96683-1442
USS WHITE PLAINS	AFS	4	96683-3033
USS WICHITA	AOR	1	96683-3023
USS WILLAMETTE	AO	180	96683-3023
USS WILLIAMS JACK	FFG	24	34093-1480
USS WILSON HENRY B	DDG	7	96683-1237
USS WILSON WOODROW	SSBN	624	34093-2018
USS WILSON WOODROW (B)	SSBN	624	34093-2019
USS WILSON WOODROW (G)	SSBN	624	34093-2020
USS WISCONSIN	BB	64	09552-1130
USS WORDEN	CG	18	96683-1142
USS YARNELL HARRY	CG	17	09594-1159
USS YELLOWSTONE	AD	41	09512-2525
USS YORKTOWN	CG	48	09594-1159

Ships Name	Hull Number	ZIP + 4 Code
USS YOSEMITE	AD 19	34083-2510
USS YOUNG JOHN	DD 973	96686-1211
B—Blue Crew	G—Gold Crew	

In July 1991 the following APOs and FPOs were changed (old numbers not listed are unchanged). Also a new system on addresses was established which replaces city names such as New York and San Francisco with a two-letter code in the last line of the address. A new mailing address to Europe might read:

Sgt. John Doe
Company A, 122 Signal Battalion
Unit 20501, Box 4290
APO AE 09795

APOs and FPOs in the Pacific area use the new two-letter code AP. A new mailing address might read:

PCCM John Doe
HI Division, Admin
USS Nimitz (CVN 88)
FPO AP 96697

APO and FPO numbers for Central or South America are unchanged, but the new code is AA.

PACIFIC

Old	New	Old	New	Old	New	Old	New
96209	96554	96351	96643	96619	96517	98763	96314
96210	96318	96356	96520	96630	96540	98764	96310
96211	96553	96358	96258	96637	96539	98765	96350
96230	96364	96361	96330	96650	96450	98766	96322
96235	96365	96366	96266	96651	96451	98767	96306
96239	96368	96369	96548	96652	96452	98768	96313
96244	96323	96371	96201	96654	96454	98769	96269
96248	96374	96397	96297	96655	96521	98770	96370
96270	96325	96404	96549	96656	96445	98772	96372
96274	96409	96405	96551	96658	96456	98773	96373
96277	96447	96455	96267	96659	96522	98774	96379
96286	96407	96460	96260	96680	96550	98775	96375
96287	96562	96461	96261	96685	96464	98776	96377
96293	96326	96483	96283	96690	96531	98777	96505
96301	96205	96488	96284	96691	96598	98778	96362
96302	96203	96501	96518	96692	96599	98780	96697
96305	96558	96502	96339	96699	96534	98781	96381
96311	96411	96503	96337	98704	96509	98782	96382
96324	96216	96604	96338	98713	96513	98783	96321
96327	96541	96519	96319	98723	96510	98791	96606
96331	96376	96524	96257	98733	96508	98796	96507
96334	96542	96628	96440	98736	96512	98798	96613
96335	96207	96570	96278	98760	96347	98799	96698
96344	96378	96571	96272	98761	96348		
96346	96546	96614	96516	98762	96349		

EUROPE and AFRICA

Old	New	Old	New	Old	New	Old	New	Old	New
09002	09618	09170	09716	09325	09263	09520	09626	09669	09206
09011	09703	09179	09464	09326	09264	09521	09619	09671	09809
09017	09802	09193	09465	09330	09265	09522	09609	09672	09830
09019	09613	09194	09466	09333	09266	09523	09627	09673	09725
09023	09704	09198	09467	09338	09826	09524	09620	09674	09839
09030	09815	09210	09468	09351	09267	09525	09847	09675	09831
09038	09803	09219	09717	09352	09268	09526	09834	09677	09832
09040	09816	09221	09630	09353	09269	09527	09835	09678	09726
09043	09732	09223	09840	09354	09270	09528	09865	09679	09833
09048	09410	09224	09821	09355	09272	09530	09836	09690	09843
09049	09447	09232	09610	09358	09273	09533	09612	09691	09810
09051	09817	09236	09469	09359	09274	09537	09622	09692	09207
09055	09705	09238	09470	09360	09275	09539	09644	09693	09844
09075	09448	09240	09605	09378	09494	09540	09645	09896	09214
09083	09449	09241	09471	09379	09838	09542	09837	09696	09222
09084	09706	09243	09472	09380	09827	09553	09421	09697	09811
09085	09707	09253	09841	09401	09647	09554	09621	09701	09225
09088	09708	09254	09822	09403	09014	09555	09625	09702	09226
09117	09818	09255	09842	09406	09720	09560	09727	09710	09228
09118	09819	09256	09845	09407	09041	09571	09728	09711	09233
09120	09450	09257	09823	09411	09044	09572	09729	09712	09234
09121	09709	09282	09643	09451	09065	09597	09730	09742	09235
09125	09456	09283	09641	09452	09071	09698	09731	09743	09237
09127	09459	09284	09718	09453	09628	09607	09495	09751	09239
09129	09461	09285	09642	09454	09073	09611	09187	09755	09497
09133	09820	09286	09646	09455	09089	09614	09812	09757	09242
09145	09713	09289	09824	09457	09096	09615	09806	09794	09624
09148	09814	09291	09846	09458	09157	09616	09808	09801	09244
09150	09462	09292	09719	09509	09498	09633	09192	09807	09248
09151	09463	09293	09601	09510	09499	09634	09196	09860	09249
09152	09804	09294	09825	09511	09415	09659	09496	09862	09721
09153	09714	09298	09805	09514	09416	09662	09828	09870	09722
09156	09813	09305	09260	09515	09422	09664	09723	09872	09251
09159	09715	09309	09890	09516	09418	09666	09202		
09161	09606	09321	09261	09518	09419	09667	09724		
09168	09629	09322	09262	09519	09420	09668	09829		

PATERNITY SUITS, CHILD SUPPORT
AND OVERSEAS MARRIAGES

For any of these matters write to the Commanding Officer of the unit to which the active duty member is assigned. Be sure to include full name, rank, SSN and organization, if known.

If the person involved is on active duty in the Army, you may get assistance by writing to:

Army Community and Family Support Center
ATTN: DACF-IS-PA
Alexandria, VA 22331-0504

AMERICAN RED CROSS

The American Red Cross has a special arrangement with the Armed Forces and usually has one or more representatives at each military installation to deal with families of military members concerning family emergencies.

To locate a member of the Armed Forces (who is on active duty or active duty for training) due to an emergency in their family, such as a death or serious illness, do not contact the military but call your local Red Cross chapter. They are listed in the telephone book. Tell the Red Cross representative the nature of the emergency and the name, rank, and service of the military member. The Red Cross will immediately investigate the matter, send a message to the military member and make arrangements for his immediate return home, if warranted. The Red Cross has certain guidelines and if these conditions are met, this is the fastest and best way to get word to someone in the military when a crisis at home exists.

ACTIVE MILITARY OWES YOU MONEY

If the person you are looking for owes you money and is on active duty with any of the Armed Forces, you should find out to what organization he is assigned, then write a letter to the Commanding Officer of his unit. Include all facts concerning the indebtedness, (i.e. amount, date, purchase, loan, the amount and dates he has made payments and current amount due, etc.).

The military does not look favorably on delinquency or avoidance of payment of legitimate debts by service members. You will receive a reply from the commanding officer who will advise ou what payments you may expect. You will most likely receive such a reply within two to three weeks.

Collection agencies cannot legally write to an individual's Commanding Officer asking for their assistance; however, they can prepare a letter for their client to an individual's Commanding Officer using the client's letterhead and signed by the client requesting assistance. The letter may state that payments be made directly to the collection agency.

CHAPTER THREE

HOW TO LOCATE MEMBERS OF THE RESERVE AND NATIONAL GUARD

The Armed Forces operates locators which will provide the unit of assignment or forward a letter to members of the reserve and National Guard. Members assigned to the inactive reserve and Individual Ready Reserve (IRR) are not assigned to a unit and the locators will only forward a letter to the members home address. (See chapter two for procedure).

TO LOCATE MEMBERS OF THE NAVY RESERVE

Navy Military Personnel Command   (202) 694-5011
World Wide Locator   (202) 694-3155
N-0216
Washington, DC 20370

The Navy locator will provide the US land based unit location of all active duty and active reserve personnel over the telephone.

TO LOCATE MEMBERS OF THE NAVY INDIVIDUAL READY RESERVE (IRR) AND INACTIVE RESERVE

Navy Reserve Personnel Center   (800) 535-2699
4400 Dauphin Street   (504) 948-5400
New Orleans, LA 70149   (504) 948-5404
(Do not put a return address on letter to be forwarded)

TO LOCATE MEMBERS OF THE ARMY RESERVE AND INACTIVE RESERVE

Army Reserve Personnel Center
ATTN: DARP-PAS-EVS
9700 Page Blvd
St. Louis, MO 63132-5100
(No research fee)

TO LOCATE MEMBERS OF THE ARMY NATIONAL GUARD

To locate members of the Army National Guard you must write to the appropriate State Adjutant General. To determine what state an officer is assigned, who is currently in the Army National Guard, call the Army National Guard Support Center (703) 756-4632. To locate personnel assigned to the National Guard Bureau call (202) 697-2943 (Army) and (202) 697-9751 (Air Force).

THE STATE ADJUTANTS GENERAL

ALABAMA
Adjutant General
P O Box 3711
Montgomery, AL 36109-0711
(205) 271-7400

ALASKA
Adjutant General
800 E. Diamond St. Ste 3-450
Anchorage, AK 99515-2097
(907) 249-1565

ARIZONA
Adjutant General
5636 E. McDowell Road
Phoenix, AZ 85008-3495
(602) 267-2710

ARKANSAS
Adjutant General
Camp Robinson
N. Little Rock, AR 72118-2200
(501) 771-5200

CALIFORNIA
Adjutant General
2829 Watt Avenue
Sacramento, CA 95821-4405
(916) 973-3500

COLORADO
Adjutant General
6868 S. Revere Pkwy Ste 200
Englewood CO 80112-6710
(303) 777-8669

CONNECTICUT
Adjutant General
360 Broad Street
Hartford, CT 06105-3795
(203) 524-4953

DELAWARE
Adjutant General
First Regiment Road
Wilmington, DE 19808-2191
(302) 324-7000

DISTRICT OF COLUMBIA
Commanding General
DC National Guard
2001 Capitol Street
Washington, DC 20003-1719
(202) 433-5220

FLORIDA
Adjutant General
State Arsenal
St. Augustine, FL 32084-1008
(904) 824-8461

GEORGIA
Adjutant General
Dept of Defense Mil.Div.
P O Box 17965
Atlanta, GA 30316-0965
(404) 624-6000

HAWAII
Adjutant General
3949 Diamond Head Road
Honolulu, HI 96816-4495
(808) 734-2195

IDAHO
Adjutant General
PO Box 45
Boise, ID 83707-0045
(208) 389-5242

ILLINOIS
Adjutant General
1301 N. MacArthur Blvd.
Springfield, IL 62702-2399
(217) 785-3500

INDIANA
Adjutant General
P O Box 41326
Indianapolis, IN 46241-0326
(317) 247-3274

IOWA
Adjutant General
7700 NW Beaver Drive
Camp Dodge
Johnston, IA 50131-1902
(515) 242-5011

KANSAS
Adjutant General
P O Box C-300
Topeka, KS 66601-0300
(913) 266-1000

KENTUCKY
Adjutant General
Boone Nat'l Guard Center
Frankfort, KY 40601-6168
(502) 564-8558

LOUISIANA
Adjutant General
Jackson Barracks, Bldg 1
New Orleans, LA 70146-0330
(504) 278-6211

MAINE
Adjutant General
Camp Keyes
Augusta, ME 04333-0033
(207) 626-9331

MARYLAND
Adjutant General
5th Regiment Armory
Baltimore, MD 21201-2288
(301) 576-6097

MASSACHUSETTS
Adjutant General
25 Haverhill Street
Reading, MA 01867-1999
(617) 944-0500

MICHIGAN
Adjutant General
2500 S. Washington Avenue
Lansing, MI 48913-5101
(517) 483-5507

MINNESOTA
Adjutant General
Veterans Service Bldg
St. Paul, MN 55155-2098
(612) 296-4666

MISSISSIPPI
Adjutant General
P O Box   139
Jackson, MS 39205
(601) 973-6232

MISSOURI
Adjutant General
1717 Industrial Drive
Jefferson City, MO 65101-1468
(314) 751-9710

MONTANA
Adjutant General
P O Box 4789
Helena, MT 59604-4789
(406) 444-6910

NEBRASKA
Adjutant General
1300 Military Road
Lincoln, NE 68508-1090
(402) 471-3241

NEVADA
Adjutant General
2525 S. Carson St.
Carson City, NV 89701-5502
(702) 887-7302

NEW HAMPSHIRE
Adjutant General
State Military Reservation
One Airport Road
Concord, NH 03301-5353
(603) 225-1200

NEW JERSEY
Adjutant General
Eggert Crossing Road CN 340
Trenton, NJ 08625-0340
(609) 292-3887

NEW MEXICO
Adjutant General
P O Box 4277
Santa Fe, NM 87502-4277
(505) 473-2402

NEW YORK
Adjutant General
330 Old Niskayuna Road
Latham, NY 12110-2224
(518) 786-4502

NORTH CAROLINA
Adjutant General
4105 Reedy Creek Road
Raleigh, NC 27607-6410
(919) 664-6101

NORTH DAKOTA
Adjutant General
P O Box 5511
Bismark, ND 58502-5511
(701) 224-5105

OHIO
Adjutant General
2825 W. Granville Road
Columbus, OH 43235-2712
(614) 889-7070

OKLAHOMA
Adjutant General
3501 Military Circle
Oklahoma City, OK 73111-4398
(405) 425-8201

OREGON
Adjutant General
PO Box 14350
Salem, OR 97309-5047
(503) 378-3980

PENNSYLVANIA
Adjutant General
Dept of Military Affairs
Annville, PA 17003-5002
(717) 865-8500

RHODE ISLAND
Adjutant General
1051 N. Main Street
Providence, RI 02904-5717
(401) 457-4100

SOUTH CAROLINA
Adjutant General
One National Guard Road
Columbia, SC 29201-3117
(803) 748-4216

SOUTH DAKOTA
Adjutant General
2835 W. Main
Rapid City, SD 57702-8186
(605) 399-6702

TENNESSEE
Adjutant General
P O Box 41502
Nashville, TN 37204-1501
(615) 252-3001

TEXAS
Adjutant General
P O Box 5218
Austin, TX 78763-5218
(512) 465-5006

UTAH
Adjutant General
P O Box 1776
Draper, UT 84020-1776
(801) 524-3900

VERMONT
Adjutant General
Camp Johnson, Bldg 1
Colchester, VT 05446
(802) 864-1124

VIRGINIA
Adjutant General
501 E. Franklin Street
Richmond, VA 23219-2317
(804) 344-4102

WASHINGTON
Adjutant General
Camp Murray
Tacoma, WA 98430-5000
(206) 581-1950

WEST VIRGINIA
Adjutant General
1703 Coonskin Drive
Charleston, WV 25311-1085
(304) 341-6316

WISCONSIN
Adjutant General
P O Box 8111
Madison, WI 53708-8111
(608) 241-6312

WYOMING
Adjutant General
PO Box 1709
Cheyenne, WY 82003-1709
(307) 772-6234

PUERTO RICO
Adjutant General
P O Box 3786
San Juan, PR 00904-3786
(809) 724-1295

GUAM
Adjutant General
622 E. Harmon Ind. Pk. Rd.
Tamuning, GU 96911-4421
(671) 632-0341

VIRGIN ISLANDS
Adjutant General
FAB Alexander Hamilton Aprt
Saint Croix, VI 00850
(809) 778-4916

STATE GUARD

Seventeen states have State Guard or Defense Organizations, which are not a part of the National Guard, but are volunteer military units that come under the jurisdiction of the State Adjutant General of the appropriate state. You must contact each state Adjutant General separately for information on their members. (See previous list for address.) Address your letter to The Adjutant General, State of _____,

The following states have State Guard organizations:

Alabama	Ohio
California	Oregon
Indiana	Puerto Rico
Louisiana	South Carolina
Maryland	Texas
Massachusetts	Utah
Nevada	Virginia
New Mexico	Washington
New York	

For additional information contact:

State Defense Force Association of US
9140 Ward Parkway
Kansas City, MO 64114

TO LOCATE MEMBERS OF THE COAST GUARD RESERVE

Commandant   (202) 267-0547
U S Coast Guard
Locator Service G-PIM-2
2100 2nd Street, S.W.
Washington, DC 20593-0001

TO LOCATE MEMBERS OF THE MARINE CORPS SELECTED RESERVE

Commandant   (703) 640-3942
Marine Corps (MMRB-10)
Locator Service
Bldg 2008
Quantico, VA 22134-0001

TO LOCATE MEMBERS OF THE MARINE CORPS INDIVIDUAL READY RESERVE AND FLEET MC RESERVE/INACTIVE RESERVE

Marine Corps Reserve Support Center
10950 El Monte   (913) 491-7502
Overland Park, KS 66211-1408

TO LOCATE MEMBERS OF THE AIR FORCE RESERVE AND AIR NATIONAL GUARD

USAF World Wide Locator   Recording (512) 652-5774
9504 IH 35 North   (512) 652-5775
San Antonio, TX 78233-6630

The Air Force locator will forward only one letter per each request and will not provide overseas unit of assignment of active members or reserve units on active duty. Requests for more than one address per letter will be returned without action. Include self-addressed stamped envelope with request for unit assignment. If the individual is separated from the Air Force they will tell you (1964 to date).

LOCATE MEMBERS OF RESERVE AND NATIONAL GUARD THROUGH THE DEPARTMENT OF VETERANS AFFAIRS

Members of the reserves and National Guard who have served on active duty in the Armed Forces are considered veterans. They may have applied for veterans benefits. Also numerous members of the Reserve Components are eligible for educational benefits under the Montgomery Act which is administered by the Department of Veterans Affairs. These individuals may also be contacted through the VA (see chapter five for details).

CIVIL AIR PATROL

The Civil Air Patrol is an official auxiliary organization of the US Air Force. Its members are civilian, but many are former and retired military. The uniform has insignias of rank that are similar to the Air Force. Send inquires to:

Civil Air Patrol
Maxwell AFB, AL 36112

CHAPTER FOUR

HOW TO LOCATE RETIRED MEMBERS

*The Armed Forces World–Wide Locators will forward letters to re-
tired members of the Armed Forces. These retired members include those
who have been retired from active duty, the reserve or National Guard.
Reserve and National Guard members do not become eligible for retired
pay until age 60. They are usually members of the inactive reserve until
they become eligible for retired pay and may be located through the
reserve (see chapter three).*

RETIRED FROM THE NAVY

ACTIVE DUTY OR RESERVE

Navy Reserve Personnel Center   (800) 535-2699
4400 Dauphin Street   (504) 948-5400
New Orleans, LA 70149
(no search fee)
Do not put a return address on letter to be forwarded.

RETIRED FROM THE ARMY

ACTIVE DUTY, ARMY RESERVE OR
ARMY NATIONAL GUARD

Army Reserve Personnel Center
ATTN: DARP-PAS-EVS   Reserve   (800) 325-8311
9700 Page Blvd   Active   (314) 538-3421
St. Louis, MO 63132-5200

RETIRED FROM THE COAST GUARD

ACTIVE DUTY OR RESERVE

Retired Military Affairs Branch G-PS-1   (202) 267-1845
US Coast Guard
Washington, DC 20593

RETIRED FROM THE MARINE CORPS

ACTIVE DUTY OR RESERVE

Commandant   (703) 640-3942
US Marine Corps
(MMSR-6)
Washington, DC 20380-0001

RETIRED FROM THE AIR FORCE

ACTIVE DUTY, AIR FORCE RESERVE OR AIR NATIONAL GUARD

USAF World Wide Locator   Recording   (512) 652 5774
9504 IH 35 North   (512) 652-5775
San Antonio, TX 78233-6636

This locator will forward only one letter per each request. Requests for more than one address per letter will be returned without action.

TO LOCATE RETIRED NATIONAL OCEANIC AND ATMOSPHERIC ADMINISTRATION PERSONNEL

Commissioned Personnel Division   (301) 443-8910
NCI N009
Rockville, MD 20852

TO LOCATE RETIRED US PUBLIC HEALTH SERVICE PERSONNEL

U.S. Public Health Service   (301) 443-3087
Department of Health and Human Services
PHS/CPOD
5600 Fishers Lane
Parklawn Bldg Room 4-35
Rockville, MD 20857

TO LOCATE RETIRED MEMBERS THROUGH RETIRED PAY CENTERS

If a locator is unable to identify the person you are looking for, you may be able to get some assistance from the appropriate service finance center.

Air Force   (800) 525-0104
Retired Pay Division
Denver, CO 80280-5000

Army   (800) 428-2290
Retired Pay Division
USAF&A
Indianapolis, IN 46249

Coast Guard   (800) 424-7950
Retired Pay Division
Pay and Personnel Center
444 S.E. Quincy St.
Topeka, KS 66683-3591

Marine Corps Finance Center   (800) 645-2024
Retired Pay Division
Kansas City, MO 64197

Navy Finance Center   (800) 321-0180
Federal Building
Retired Pay
Cleveland, OH 44199-2058

TO LOCATE WIDOWS/WIDOWERS OF MILITARY RETIREES

Some addresses of widows/widowers of military personnel who retired from the Armed Forces (active duty, reserves and National Guard) may be contained in the files of the individual service if they are receiving survivor's benefits from that particular service. Not all widows/widowers receive these benefits, therefore their address would not be listed. If the person is a recipient of these benefits, the Privacy Act prohibits releasing their address, but the service may forward a letter as they will for retirees. For more information contact the appropriate finance center. The addresses and telephone numbers are listed in the preceding section.

TO LOCATE DIVORCED SPOUSES OF ACTIVE AND RETIRE MEMBERS

Some divorced spouses of active duty and retired military members may be eligible for some military privileges, such as commissary, exchange and medical benefits. Normally these spouses were married at least twenty years or more to someone who was on active duty at least twenty years. You may have a letter forwarded to them in the same manner as mentioned for military members. Call or write to determine if the individual is listed in the Defense Enrollment Eligibility Reporting System (DEERS) automated files. The DEERS file contains the names and addresses of all dependents and former dependents of active duty and retired personnel eligible for military benefits. It also contains the names and addresses of all retired members.

DEERS Support Office		(800) 538-9525
2511 Garden Road, A260	CA	(800) 334-4162
ATTN: Field Support	AK,HI	(800) 527-5602
Monterey, CA 93940		

RETIREMENT SERVICES OFFICERS

Most major military installations have retirement services/retiree activity officers who assist military retirees of all military services in providing information on retired benefits and services. These officers deal closely with the retired military population and may be able to provide some assistance in locating retired members in their service areas. Call the base/post information operator for their telephone number (see chapter two).

CHAPTER FIVE

HOW TO LOCATE VETERANS OF THE ARMED FORCES AND FORMER MEMBERS OF THE RESERVE AND NATIONAL GUARD

This chapter explains how to locate veterans and former members of the Reserve Components through the Departments of Veterans Affairs, The National Personnel Records Center, Veterans Organizations, Military Reunion Organizations, and private organizations.

DEPARTMENT OF VETERANS AFFAIRS

The Department of Veterans Affairs (formerly the Veterans Administration) will forward a letter in a similar manner as the Armed Forces. (see chapter two) Before attempting to have a letter forwarded it is recommended that you call the VA Regional Office closest to you. See the list below for toll free telephone numbers. Tell the VA counselor that you wish to verify that a veteran is listed in their files before you mail any correspondence. Give the individual's full name and service number, social security number or VA file or claim number, if known. If you do not have this information the VA can sometimes identify veterans with either their date of birth, city and state that the person entered the service, branch of service, middle name or possibly the name alone, if the person has a unique name. If the individual's name is listed in the files, ask for their VA claim number.

If the Regional Office cannot find the individual in their file then contact the VA Insurance Office in Philadelphia at:

Department of Veterans Affairs   800-669-8477
PO Box 13399
Philadelphia, PA 19101

This office has insurance information in its files which is not readily available in the regional offices files.

The VA does not have all veterans listed in their files; only those individuals who have at some time applied for VA benefits, such as educational assistance, disability compensation, pensions, home loans, and VA insurance. The address in their file is the address when the veteran last obtained or applied for VA benefits. To have a letter forwarded, place your correspondence in an unsealed, stamped envelope without your return address. Put the veteran's name and VA file number on the front of the envelope. Next prepare a short fact sheet and state that you request the VA forward this letter to the veteran. Tell them you were given the VA claim number by their Regional Office. Also include all other pertinent information to insure they can identify the veteran. Include as much information as you can such as name, service number, SSN, date of birth, city and state entered service, etc. Next place this letter and the fact sheet in a larger envelope and mail to the VA Regional Office you spoke with, or where that office instructed you to send it. If they cannot identify the individual, they will return your letter to you. They will also inform you if the letter is undeliverable by the Post Office. The VA is very cooperative in providing assistance in locating veterans. There are over 27 million living veterans. There are approximately 100,000 veterans of World War I, more than nine million veterans of World War II, almost five million veterans of the Korean War and more than eight million veterans of the war in Vietnam are still living.

VA REGIONAL OFFICES

ALABAMA	**ALASKA**	**ARIZONA**
474 S. Court Street	235 E. 8th Avenue	3225 N Central Ave
Montgomery, AL 36104	Anchorage, AK 99501	Phoenix, AZ 85012
(800) 392-8054	(800) 478-2500	(800) 352-0451
ARKANSAS	**CALIFORNIA**	**CALIFORNIA**
PO Box 1280	Federal Building	2022 Cam. Del Norte
N. Little Rock,AR 72215	11000 Wilshire Blvd	San Diego, CA 92108
(800) 482-5434	W. LA, CA 90024	(800) 532-3811
	(800) 648-5406	
CALIFORNIA	**COLORADO**	**CONNECTICUT**
211 Main Street	P O Box 25126	450 Main Street
San Francisco,CA 94105	Denver, CO 80225	Hartford, CT 06103
(800) 652-1240	(800) 332-6742	(800) 842-4315

DELAWARE
1601 Kirkwood Hwy
Wilmington, DE 19805
(800) 292-7855

DISTRICT OF
COLUMBIA
941 N Capitol NE
Washington, DC 20421
(800) 872-1151

FLORIDA
144 1st Avenue South
St Petersburg,
FL 33701
(800) 827-2204

GEORGIA
730 Peachtree St. N.E.
Atlanta, GA 30365
(800) 282-0232

HAWAII
P O Box 50188
Honolulu, HI 96850
(800) 232-2535

IDAHO
550 W Fort St.
Boise, ID 83724
(800) 632-2003

ILLINOIS
P O Box 8136
Chicago, IL 60680
(800) 972-5327

INDIANA
575 N Pennsylvania St
Indianapolis, IN 46294
(800) 382-4540

IOWA
810 Walnut Street
Des Moines, IA 50309
(800) 362-2222

KANSAS
901 George Washington
Wichita, KS 67211
(800) 362-2444

KENTUCKY
600 Martin L. King Jr.
Louisville, KY 40202
(800) 292-4562

LOUISIANA
701 Loyola Avenue
New Orleans
LA 70113
(800) 462-9510

MAINE
Togus, ME 04330
(800) 452-1935

MARYLAND
31 Hopkins Plaza
Baltimore, MD 21201
(800) 492-9503

MASSACHUSETTS
JF Kennedy Fed Bldg
Boston, MA 02203
(800) 392-6015

MICHIGAN
477 Michigan Avenue
Detroit, MI 48226
(800) 827-1966

MINNESOTA
Fed Bldg, Ft. Snelling
St. Paul, MN 55111
(800) 692-2121

MISSISSIPPI
100 W. Capitol Street
Jackson, MS 39269
(800) 682-5270

MISSOURI
2520 Market Street
St. Louis, MO 63103
(800) 392-3761

MONTANA
Ft Harrison,MT 59636
(800) 332-6125

NEBRASKA
100 Cent. Mall North
Lincoln, NE 68508
(800) 742-7554

NEVADA
1201 Terminal Way
Reno, NV 89520
(800) 992-5740

NEW HAMPSHIRE
275 Chestnut Street
Manchester, NH 03101
(800) 562-5260

NEW JERSEY
20 Washington Place
Newark, NJ 07102
(800) 242-5867

NEW MEXICO
500 Gold Avenue S.W.
Albuquerque,NM 87102
(800) 432-6853

NEW YORK
111 W. Huron Street
Buffalo, NY 14202
(800) 462-1130

NEW YORK
252 7th Ave/24th St.
NY City, NY 10001
(800) 442-5882

NORTH CAROLINA
251 N. Main Street
Winston, NC 27155
(800) 642-0841

NORTH DAKOTA
655 First Ave, North
Fargo, ND 58102
(800) 342-4790

OHIO
1240 E. 9th Street
Cleveland, OH 44199
(800) 827-8272

OKLAHOMA	OREGON	PENNSYLVANIA
125 S. Main Street	1220 SW 3rd Avenue	P O Box 8079
Muskogee, OK 74401	Portland, OR 97204	Phil., PA 19101
(800) 482-2800	(800) 452-7276	(800) 822-3920
PENNSYLVANIA	PUERTO RICO	RHODE ISLAND
1000 Liberty Avenue	GPO Box 4867	380 Westminster Mall
Pittsburgh, PA 15222	San Juan, PR 00936	Providence, RI 02903
(800) 242-0233	(800) 462-4135	(800) 322-0230
SOUTH CAROLINA	SOUTH DAKOTA	TENNESSEE
1801 Assembly Street	P O Box 5046	110 9th Street
Columbia, SC 29201	Sioux Falls, SD 57117	Nashville, TN 37203
(800) 922-1000	(800) 952-3550	(800) 342-8330
TEXAS	TEXAS	UTAH
2515 Murworth Drive	1400 N.Valley Mills Dr	P O Box 11500
Houston, TX 77054	Waco, TX 76799	S.Lake City,UT 84147
(800) 392-2200	(800) 827-2012	(800) 662-9163
VERMONT	VIRGINIA	WASHINGTON
White River Junction,	210 Franklin Rd S.W.	915 2nd Avenue
Vermont 05001	Roanoke, VA 24011	Seattle, WA 98174
(800) 622-4134	(800) 542-5826	(800) 552-7480
WEST VIRGINIA	WISCONSIN	WYOMING
640 Fourth Avenue	5000 W. National Ave	2360 E. Pershing Blvd
Huntington, WV 25701	Building 6	Cheyenne, WY 82001
(800) 642-3520	Milwaukee, WI 53298	(800) 442-2761
	(800) 242-9025	

The 800 toll free numbers listed above can only be used from within the state that the Regional Office is located. Include VA REGIONAL OFFICE as the first line in each of these addresses when writing.

MAILING FROM A ROSTER

The VA Records Processing Center in St. Louis, Missouri, (do not confuse this office with the National Personnel Records Center which is also located in St Louis, MO) is responsible for research of rosters so people can forward letters to large groups of veterans, such as a military unit reunion notification or to several veterans to secure statements to substantiate VA disability claims. Anyone may use this service whether a veteran or not. There are two ways to use the VA Records Processing Center. First, you can submit a roster of veterans names and service numbers (see section on unit or ship's rosters), or one of the following if you do not have a service number to help identify the veteran:

a. Social Security number
b. VA file or claim number
c. Date of birth
d. Place of entry into service (city and state)
e. Middle name
f. Name only (if veteran has a unique name)
g. Branch of service

Include a check or money order for $2.00 for each name to be researched, made payable to the Department of Veterans Affairs (personal checks are acceptable). The center will research the names and provide you a list of each name submitted with the following information:

a. VA file or claim number
b. VA folder location (VA Regional Office)
c. If the veteran is deceased and date of . . death, if known.
d. If the VA does not have a record, they will notify you of this. (veteran has never applied for VA benefits.)
e. If they cannot identify the veteran from the information provided.

The VA file number is sometimes referred to as the VA claim number and may be in some cases the same as the veterans service number or Social Security number. Since June 1974 the VA has used Social Security numbers as VA Claim numbers. Claim number in this category will have the letter "C" followed by the nine digit SSN without any dashes or spaces.

The list will be returned to you along with instructions on how to have letters forwarded to these veterans. The letters should be submitted with the VA claim number listed along with the name on an unsealed envelope, with sufficient postage to cover mailing costs, and with no return address. No letters involving debt collections will be forwarded.

The VA cannot assure that the veteran will either receive or respond to this correspondence. If the letter is returned to the VA by the Post Office as undeliverable, the inquirer will be notified approximately five weeks after the letter is mailed.

The second way to use this center's service is by sending the letters, rosters and payments together. The center will do the necessary research and forward the letters. This process usually takes up to two weeks to complete. Send rosters and payment or rosters, letters and payment to:

VA Records Processing Center
Post Office Box 5020
St. Louis, MO 6311

THE NATIONAL PERSONNEL RECORDS CENTER

The National Personnel Records Center (NPRC) will forward correspondence to veterans to their last known address (address in their military records when the individual separated from active duty or when his reserve commitment was completed) only in limited situations. These include:

a. Requestor's VA/Social Security benefits are dependent on contacting the veteran.
b. Veteran to be contacted will have veterans benefits affected.
c. Forwarding is in veteran's/next of kin's interest e.g.
  estate settlement
d. Financial institution's legitimate effort to collect a debt.

A search fee of $3.50 is applicable only when the forwarding of correspondence is not in the veteran's interest, e.g. debt collection. Make checks payable to "Treasurer of the US."

The NPRC will place the letter to be forwarded in another envelope and will add the individual's name and last known address. In the event the letter is not delivered, it will be returned to the NPRC and you will not be informed.

A federal court decision in 1990 directed the NPRC to forward letters to the last known address of veterans who may have fathered illegitimate children who are members of "War Babes" or similarly situated individuals. (War Babes is an organization of children fathered by US servicemen while in Great Britain during WW II.)

If a person writes to the NPRC for assistance in locating a veteran and the reason does not fall into any of the above categories, then the writer will be informed to contact the nearest VA Regional Office (for requests of fewer than five names) or the VA Records Processing Center (for requests of five or more names). Requests should have the name,

SSN, service number or VA claim number. See preceding sections for details.

In July, 1973 a fire at the NPRC destroyed about 80% of the records for Army personnel discharged between November 1, 1912 and January 1, 1960. About 75% of the records for Air Force personnel with surnames from Hubbard through "Z" who were discharged between September 25, 1947 and January 1, 1964 were also destroyed. Some alternate information may be obtained from records of the State Adjutants General and State "Veterans Service" offices. There are currently 48 million military records at the NPRC.

National Personnel Records Center
9700 Page Blvd   (314) 263-3901
St. Louis, MO 63132-5100

SELECTIVE SERVICE RECORDS

The classification records of individuals who were registered under the Selective Service Act and information from ledger books are available to the public. These classification records list name, date of birth, draft classification, date to report for induction and in some cases date of separation. Records were maintained from 1940 to 1975. These records are maintained at various federal records centers (by state and county). All requests for information, if available, must be made through:

National Headquarters
Selective Service System   (202) 724-0820
Washington, DC 20435

TO LOCATE CIVIL SERVICE EMPLOYEES

Thousands of former (veterans) and retired military are employed by the federal Civil Service because of military experience and hiring preference. To determine if a person is employed by the federal Civil Service you must contact each federal agency separately since there is no central locator service for current Civil Service employees. You may have letters forwarded to retired members of the Civil Service by sending your letters to the following address:

Office of Personnel Management   (412) 794-3141
Employee Service and Records Center
Boyer, PA 16017

You may locate Civil Service personnel or non-appropriated fund civilian personnel (civilian who works for military clubs, messes and exchanges) who are employed at military bases by calling the appropriate base assistance operator and asking for the telephone number of the Civilian Locator. (See Base/Post Locator, chapter two, for telephone numbers). These locators will provide work assignment and work telephone number.

TO LOCATE FORMER MERCHANT MARINERS

The Merchant Marines is a civil organization and refers to the nation's commercial shipping industry. It is not an Armed or Uniformed Service of the United States. However, many Merchant Mariners and Officers are members of the Navy, Coast Guard, and Army reserves. Graduates of the US Merchant Marine Academy at Kings Point, New York are appointed officers in the US Navy Reserve. You may locate them through the appropriate military reserve. The US Coast Guard registers all merchant seamen and can be contacted at the following address.

Commandant (GMVP 1/12)
US Coast Guard
Washington, DC 20593-0001

or contact the following:

American Merchant Marine Veterans
905 Cape Coral Parkway
Cape Coral, FL 33904

or

US Merchant Marine
Veterans of World War II
PO Box 629
San Pedro, CA 90731

In January 1988, a Federal court decision awarded veteran status to all merchant seamen who served in World War II (December 7, 1941 to

August 15, 1945), so you may attempt to contact members of this group of Merchant Mariners through the Department of Veterans Affairs.

Merchant Mariners must apply for a military discharge (DD 214) before than can apply for veterans benefits. This status does not qualify them for membership in some veterans organizations such as the VFW.

VETERANS, MILITARY, AND PATRIOTIC ORGANIZATIONS

Veterans, military, and patriotic organizations can help in locating veterans and providing information about reunions of former military organizations. The service and assistance varies with each organization. Most have magazines or newsletters which publish names of veterans that people are trying to locate and dates that military unit reunions are being held.

The addresses and telephone numbers of the majority of the national organizations are listed below. When you contact them list as much information as you know such as: names, aliases, date of birth, dates of service, rank, service or SSN (see sample letter following this section). All listed organizations (except The American Legion) will provide locator service and/or will forward letters to present and former members. Usually there are no fees required for these services.

Name/ Address	Telephone Numbers	No. of Members
Air Force Association 1501 Lee Highway Arlington, Va 22209-1198	(703) 247-5810	220,000
Air Force Sergeants Association PO Box 50 Temple Hill, MD 20748	(301) 899-3500	162,000
American Red Cross 17th and D Street NW Washington, DC 20006	(202) 639-3586	N/A
American Ex-Prisoners of War, Inc. 3201 East Pioneer Parkway Suite 40 Arlington, TX 76010	(817) 649-2979	33,000

Name/ Address	Telephone Numbers	No. of Members
American Defenders of Bataan and Corregidor, Inc. PO Box 2052 New Bern, NC 28561	(919) 637-4033	3,883
American G.I. Forum of the US 1017 N Main Ste 207 San Antonio, TX 78212	(512) 233-1679	143,000
American Legion, The 700 North Pennsylvania Street P O Box 1955 Indianapolis, IN 46206	(317) 635-8411	3,000,000
American Military Members Assn. 8603 Crownhill Ste 28 San Antonio, TX 78216		6,200
American Military Retirees Assn. 68 Clinton St. Plattsburg, NY 12901	(518) 563-9479	25,00
American Veterans of World War II, Korea and Vietnam (AMVETS) 4647 Forbes Blvd. Lanham, MD 20706	(301) 459-9600	250,000
American Veterans Committee 1717 Massachusetts Ave, NW Suite 203 Washington, DC 20036	(202) 667-0090	15,000
Army and Air Force Mutual Aid Association Fort Myer Bldg 468 Arlington, VA 22211	(703) 522-3060	55,000
Army and Navy Union,U.S.A., Inc 1391 Main Street Lakemore, OH 44250	(216) 456-7312	11,000
Army Warrant Officers Assn of US P O Box 2040 Reston, VA 22090	(703) 620-3986	5,000
Association of the U.S. Army 2425 Wilson Blvd Arlington, VA 22201	(703) 841-4300	150,000

Name/ Address	Telephone Numbers	No. of Members
Blinded Veterans Association 477 H Street, NW Washington, DC 20001	(202) 371-8880	6,300
Catholic War Veterans USA 419 N Lee St. Alexandria, VA 22314	(703) 549-3622	35,000
Congressional Medal of Honor Society of the USA Intrepid Sea-Air-Space Museum 12th Ave at West 46th St New York, NY 10036	(212) 582-5355	221
Disabled American Veterans P O Box 14301 Cincinnati, OH 45250	(606) 441-7300	1,050,734
Fleet Reserve Association 1303 New Hampshire Ave, NW Washington, DC 20036	(202) 785-2768	153,000
Gold Star Wives of America 7209 N. Hammond Oklahoma City, OK 73132	(405) 721-6321	11,000
Italian American War Veterans of US 115 S Meridian Road Youngstown, OH 44509	(312) 445-4057	600
Jewish War Veterans of the USA 1811 R St, NW Washington, DC 20009	(202) 265-6280	100,00
Marine Corps Association P O Box 1775 Quantico, VA 22134	(703) 640-6161	110,000
Marine Corps League P O Box 3070 Arlington, VA 22116	(703) 207-9588	30,000
Military Chaplains Assn PO Box 42660 Washington, DC 20015		1,500
Military Order of the Purple Heart of the USA, Inc. 5413-B Backlick Road Springfield, VA 22151	(703) 642-5360	20,000

Name/ Address	Telephone Numbers	No. of Members
Military Order of the World Wars, The 435 N. Lee Street Alexandria, VA 22314	(703) 683-4911	18,000
National American Military Retirees Assn 68 Clinton Street Plattsburg, NY 12901	(518) 563-9479	25,000
National Amputation Foundation, Inc. 12-45 150th Street Whitestone, NY 11357	(718) 767-0596	2,500
National Assn for Uniformed Services 5535 Hempstead Way Springfield, VA 22151	(703) 750-1342	55,000
National Association of Atomic Veterans P O Box 3139 Independence, MO 64055	(816) 737-9434	4,000
National Assn of Women Veterans P O Box 10114 Atlanta, GA 30319	(404) 262-7870	80,000
National League of Families of American Prisoners and Missing in Southeast Asia 1001 Connecticut Ave NW Suite 219 Washington, DC 20036	(202) 223-6846	3,600
National Military Family Assn 2666 Military Road Arlington, VA 22207	(703) 841-0462	5,700
Naval Enlisted Reserve Association 6703 Farragut Avenue Falls Church, VA 22042	(703) 534-1329	16,000
Navy League of the US 2300 Wilson Blvd Arlington, VA 22201	(703) 528-1775	73,000
Navy Mutual Aid Association Arlington Annex Room G-070 Washington, DC 20370	(202) 694-1638	72,000

Name/ Address	Telephone Numbers	Num. of Members
Naval Reserve Association 1619 King Street Alexandria, VA 23314-2793	(703) 548-5800	25,000
Non Commissioned Officers Assn of the U.S.A 10635 IH35 North San Antonio, TX 78233	(512) 653-6161	160,000
Paralyzed Veterans of America 801 18th Street NW Washington, DC 20006	(202) 872-1300	14,500
Pearl Harbor Survivors Assn, Inc. 3215 Albert Street Orlando, FL 32806	(407) 648-2122	10,750
Polish Legion of American Veterans of U.S.A. 5413-C Backlick Rd. Springfield, VA 22151	(312) 283-9161	15,000
Regular Veterans Association of the US, Inc. 2470 Cardinal Loop Bldg 219 Del Valley, TX 78617	(512) 389-2288	15,811
Reserve Officers Association of the United States One Constitution Ave, NE Washington, DC 20002	(202) 479-2200	120,000
Retired Enlisted Association 14305 East Alameda Ave Suite 300 Aurora, CO 80012	(303) 364-8737	50,000
Retired Officers Association, The 201 N. Washington Street Alexandria, VA 22314-2529	(703) 549-2311	363,000
US Submarine Veterans of World War II 862 Chatham Avenue Elmhurst, IL 60126	(807) 834-2718	8,000
US Coast Guard CPO Association 5520 G Hempstead Way Springfield, VA 22151	(703) 941-0395	9,000

Name/ Address	Telephone Numbers	Num. of Members
USCG Chief Warrant and Warrant Officers Assn C/O Ft Myer Yacht Basin 200 V Street Washington, DC 20024		3,261
Veterans of World War I of the U.S.A., Inc. 941 N Capitol Street Room 1202-C Washington, DC 20002	(202) 275-1388	100,000
Veterans of Foreign Wars of the US 406 W 34th Street Kansas City, MO 64111	(816) 756-3390	2,300,000
Veterans of the Vietnam War, Inc. 2090 Bald Mountain Road Wilkes-Barre, PA 18702	(800) VIETNAM	32,500
Vietnam Veterans of America, Inc. 1224 M Street, NW Washington, DC 20005-5183	(202) 332-2700	40,137
Women's Army Corps Veterans Assn. 6313 Perry St Anniston, AL 36206	(205) 820-3218	3,300
Women in Military Service for America Memorial Foundation, Inc. Department 560 Washington, DC 20042-0560	(703) 533-1155 (800) 222-2294	15,000

SAMPLE LETTER

December 7, 1991
111 Main Street
Anytown, USA 12345
(555) 555-5555

Veteran Organization
111 Some Street
Sometown, USA 54321

Ladies/Gentlemen:

The purpose of this letter is to ask your assistance in locating my brother, John Paul Smith. I have not seen or heard from him in five years. It is extremely important that I contact him. John was born on January 1, 1939. He served in the US Navy from 1959 to 1964 as a Chief Petty Officer. He was a member of the Naval Reserve from 1964 to 1968. In 1968 he was appointed a Warrant Officer in the Transportation Corps of the US Army. His SSN is 444-44-4444. I would appreciate if you would check your files and determine if he was or is a member of your organization. If so, please advise me of his current address. If your policy prohibits giving out his address, please forward this letter to him.

If you do not have any records of his membership, would you please include a notice in your magazine or newsletter stating that I am trying to locate him or anyone who knows his location.

Thank you for your assistance.

Sincerely,

Mary Smith

TO LOCATE VETERANS
THROUGH REGISTRIES

There are several veterans registries that are operated by private organizations or individuals. The success rate for locating veterans is very low for these registries compared to other methods mentioned in this book.

The Vietnam Veterans Registry, Inc. helps to locate veterans of the Vietnam war. First, you have to register by sending a self-addressed stamped envelope. Once registered you will be notified if there is any information available on an individual so that you can send a letter to be forwarded to the person you seek. This service is free and has over 25,000 veterans listed. Send business size-self addressed stamped envelope with request for information or for a registration form.

Vietnam Veterans Registry, Inc.
P O Box 430
Collinsville, CT 06022

The Veterans Alumni Association offers a locator service to reunite members who served together but have lost contact since leaving the military. 263,000 names are registered. To guarantee that information in the computer data bank remains confidential, the member who is the object of the search will have the option of responding to the initiator of the search. For more information contact the association. There is a $3.00 membership fee and a $1.00 fee for each search.

Veterans Alumni Association
404 S. Galloway
Mesquite, TX 75149

The Vietnam Veterans Locator Service has a computer base with over 40,000 names of veterans, parents and nurses who are looking for information or who want to contact other veterans they served with. This free service also provides information on those listed as missing in action. Send the person's name, nickname and any unit information you have to the above address.

Vietnam Locator Service
7303 Volqueardsen
Davenport, LA 52806

Information Up maintains several databases by actively searching out veterans of all branches and eras, associations, reunion groups and support groups. Currently it has the addresses of 50,000 people and access to public records of 50,000 or more. To make a request or to be listed write:

Information Up   (608) 246-2045
Veterans Locator and Resource Center
4614 Hamlet Place
Madison, WI 53714

MILITARY REUNION ASSOCIATIONS

US Marine Corps Associations

1st Marine Div Assn
7622 Highland St
Springfield, VA 22191

2nd Marine Div Assn
P O Box 532756
Grand Prairie, TX 75053

3rd Marine Div Assn
2121 Skyview Glen
Escondido, CA 92027

4th Marine Div Assn
101 W. Cedarwood Cir.
Kissimmee, FL 34743

5th Marine Div Assn
340 Marshal Street
Steelton, PA 17113

6th Marine Div Assn
1106 Black Creek Rd
Devine, TX 78016

Edson's Raiders Assn
(1st Raider Bn)
P O Box 980
Washington, DC 20044

Marine Corps Assn
Box 1775
Quantico, VA 22134

Marine Corps Aviation Assn
P O Box 296
Bldg 715
Quantico, VA 22134

Marine Corps Combat
Correspondents Assn
1035 Hazen Drive
San Marcos, CA 92110

Marine Corps Mustang Assn
8425 Shern Drive Apt #402
San Antonio, TX 78216

MC Reserve Officers Assn
201 N Washington St #206
Alexandria, VA 22314

Marine Drill Instructor Assn
5458 Burford Street
San Diego, CA 92111

Marine Military Academy
320 Iwo Jima
Harlingen, TX 78550

Montford Point Marine Assn
P O Box 5865
Takoma Park, MD 20912

Retired Marine Corps
Musicians Assn
100 Domain Drive
Exeter, NH 03833

The Chosen Few
P O Box 1419
Oviedo FL 32765

US Marine Raider Assn
4119 43 Ave W
Bradenton, FL 34205

Women Marine Assn
P O Box 387
Quantico, VA 22134

WWII
Marine Parachute Units
P O Box 1972
La Jolla, CA 92038

US Army Unit Associations

11th Airborne Div Assn
14 Deer Meadows
Canyon Lake, TX 78130

17th Airborne Div Assn
62 Forty Acres Mt Road
Danbury, CT 06811

82nd Airborne Div Assn
P O Box 1442
Bloomington, ID 47402

101st Airborne Div Assn
P O Box 586
Sweetwater, TN 37874

Society of 173rd ABB
P O Box 46105
Pentagon Station
Washington, DC 20050

1st Armored Div Assn
P O Box 5675
Anderson, SC 29623

2nd Armored Div Assn
P O Box 2158
West Covina, CA 92793

3rd Armored Div Assn
P O Box 740665
New Orleans, LA 70174

4th Armored Div Assn
1823 Shady Drive
Farrell, PA 16121

5th Armored Div Assn
13344 Luthman Road
Minster, OH 45865

6th Armored Div Assn
P O Box 5011
Louisville, KY 40205

7th Armored Div Assn
23218 Springbrook Drive
Farmington Hills, MI 48024

8th Armored Div Assn
180 N. LaSalle St
Chicago, IL 60601

9th Armored Div
510 Cave Lane
San Antonio, TX 78209

10th Armored Div Assn
2525 Bucklodge Road
Adelphi, MD 20783

11th Armored Div Assn
2328 Admiral Street
Aliquippa, PA 15001

12th Armored Div Assn
4701 N. Cleveland
Kansas City, MO 64117

13th Armored Div Assn
1562 Champlin Drive
St Louis, MO 63136

14th Armored Div Assn
1001 Robin Road
Muscatine, IA 52761

16th Armored Div Assn
8-329 Road P3-R5
Napoleon, OH 43545

20th Armored Div Assn
317 Sky Hill Road, A
Alexandria, VA 23314

1st Cavalry Div Assn
302 North Main Street
Copperas Cove, TX 76522

9th & 10th Cav Regiments
2602 Agnes
Kansas City, MO 64127

11th Army Cav Vets of
Viet Nam and Cambodia
1602 Lorrie Drive
Richardson, TX 75080

11th Armored Cav Regiment
P O Box 11
Ft Knox, KY 40121

Society of the 1st Div
5 Montgomery Avenue
Philadelphia, PA 19118

2nd (Indian Head) Div Assn
P O Box 460
Buda, TX 78610

Society of the 3rd Inf Div
713 Braemere
Boise, ID 83703

National 4th Inf Div Assn
161 Vista Hermosa Circle
Sarasota, FL 34242

Society of the 5th Div
170 Evergreen
Elmhurst, IL 60126

Natl Assn of 6th Inf Div
5649 South 39th ave
Minneapolis, MN 55417

7th Inf Div Assn
3001 Richmond Avenue
Mattoon, IL 61938

9th Inf Div Assn (American)
P O Box 33342
Ft Lewis, WA 98433

10th Mt Div Assn
15W761 Butterfield Road
Elmhurst, IL 60126

23rd Inf Div Assn
247 Willow Street
West Roxbury, MA 02132

24th Inf Div Assn
120 Maple St Room 207
Springfield, MA 01103

25th Inf Div Assn
31 Beach Road
Great Neck, NY 11023

26th Div Vet Assn
74 Argyle Street
Melrose, MA 02176

27th Inf Div Assn
5 Rosewood Ave
Johnstown, NY 12095

28th Inf Div Assn.
14th and Calder
Harrisburg, PA 17103

29th Inf Div Assn
305 Northwest Dr
Silver Springs, MD 20901

30th Inf Div Assn
13645 Whippet Way East
Delray Beach, FL 33484

31st Inf Div Assn
Route 1 Box 300
Ragely, LA 70657

32nd Div Vet Assn
505 West 30th St C-3
Holland, MI 49423

33rd Div Assn
PO Box 532 3
Kirkland, WA 98083

34th Inf Div Assn
113 Aspen Ave
Richmond, VA 23228

35th Inf Div Assn
P O Box 5004
Topeka, KS 66605

36th Inf Div Assn
11017 Pandora Drive
Houston, TX 77013

37th Div Vet Assn
65 S Front St, Rm 707
Columbus, OH 43215

40th Inf Div Assn
210 Highland Avenue
Maybrook, NY 12543

41st In Div Assn
4324 175th SW
Lynwood, WA 98037

42nd (Rainbow Div) Vets
3389 Kingston Lane
Youngstown, OH 44511

43rd Inf Div Vets Assn
150 Lakedel dr
E Greenwich, RI 02818

45th Div Assn
2145 Northeast 36th St
Oklahoma City, OK 73111

53rd Inf Div
1820 Second Street
Wasco, CA 93280

63rd Inf Div Assn
19W 565 Deerpath
Lemont, IL 60439

65th Inf Div Ass
123 Dorchester Road
Buffalo, NY 14213

66th Inf Div Assn
26 East Curtis Street
Linden, NJ 07036

69th Inf Div Assn
101 Stephen Street
New Kensington, PA 15068

70th Inf Div Assn
203 S Major
Eureka, IL 61530

71st Div Vets Assn
14801 Grapeland Avenue
Cleveland, OH 44111

75th Div Vets Assn
6545 W 11th Street
Indianapolis, IN 46214

76th Inf Div Assn
Rd #2 Jackson Avenue
New Windsor, NY 12550

77th Inf Div Assn
346 Broadway Rm 816
New York, NY 10013

78th Div Vets Assn
3131 Saralake Drive
Sarasota, FL 34239

80th Div Vets Assn
527 Dixie Drive
Pittsburgh, PA 15235

81st Inf Div Reunion
2842 S Emerald Avenue
Chicago, IL 60610

83rd Inf Div Assn
3749 Spalheber Road
Hamilton, OH 45013

84th Inf Div Society
P O Box 1524
Englewood, FL 34295

86th Inf Div Assn
5328 E Calle Redondo
Phoenix, AZ 85018

87th Inf Div Assn
1014 E Boulevard
Aurora, OH 44202

88th Inf Div Assn
P O Box 925
Havertown, PA 19083

89th Inf Div Society
P O Box 489
Donnelly, ID 83615

90th Inf Div Assn
1017 N 40th Street,SW
Ft Smith, AR 72904

91st Inf Div Assn
834 Neal Avenue
Salina, KS 67401

92nd Inf Div Assn
7822 16th Street
Washington, DC 20012

93rd Inf Div Assn
2448 E Washington St
Stockton, CA 95205

96th Inf Div Assn
6723 CR #11
Risingsun, OH 43457

99th Inf Div Assn
P O Box 99
Marion, KS 66861

100th Inf Div Assn
51 Ninth Street
Carbondale, PA 18407

102nd Inf Div Assn
211 Reynard
Bridewater, NJ 08807

103rd Inf Div Assn
8260 Moreland Road
Jerome, MI 49249

104th Inf Div Assn
721 Byron Ave
New York, NY 11010

106th Inf Div Assn
474 Federal Street NW
Warren, OH 44483

American Div Vet Assn
247 Willow St.
West Roxburry, MA 02132

Army Aviation Assn
49 Richmondville Ave
Westport, CT 06880

Army OCS Alumni Assn
P O Box 2192
Ft Benning, GA 31905

International Assn of
Airborne Vets
606 West Barry Street, Suite 181
Chicago, IL 60657

Retired Army Nurse
Corps Assn
P O Box 39235
San Antonio, TX 78218

Society of Daughters of
the US Army
5840 Lowell Ave
Alexandria, VA 22313

US Navy and Coast Guard Associations

American Battleship Assn
P O Box 11247
San Diego, CA 92111

Assn of Naval Aviation
5205 Leesburg Pike
Suite 2
Falls Church, VA 22042

Coast Guard SEA Veterans -
Mid-America
18 Golf Road
Clarendon Hills, IL 60514

Destroyer Escort Sailors Assn
P O Box 680085
Orlando, FL 32868

Navy Armored Guard Vets
28 Graiam Place
Rockway Point, NY 11697

Navy Seabee Vets
Box 190
Forest Hill, LA 71430

Patrol Craft Sailors Assn
P O Box 232
Cambridge, NY 12816

Patrol Frigate Sailors Assn
5272 Dorris Drive
Arnold, MO 63010

PT Boats, Inc.
P O Box 38070
Memphis, TN 38183

Tin Can Sailors
Battleship Cove
Fall River, MA 02721

US LST Assn
P O Box 8769
Toledo, OH 43623

US Navy Memorial Foundation
Box 48817
Arlington, VA 22209-8728

WAVES National
104 Windcliffe Dr
Ballwin, MO 63021

Air Force and Army Air Force Associations

2nd Air Div Assn
P O Drawer B
Ipswich, MA 01938

8th AF Clearing House
P O Box 669
Beverly Hill, FL 32665

8th AF Historical Assn
P O Box 3556
Hollywood, FL 33083

11th Air Force Reunion
615 Stedman Street
Ketchikan, AK 99901

15th AF Assn
PO Box 6325
March AFB, CA 92518

AF Retired Nurses Society
P O Box 681026
San Antonio, TX 79257

B-26 Marauders
Historical Society
P O Box 1051
Columbia, MO 65205

Bombardiers, Inc.
200 Van Buren St #209
Dalphne, AL 36526

Caterpillar Assn
P O Box 235
Punta Gorda, FL 33951

CBI Hump Pilots Assn
808 Lester Rd
Popular Buff, MO 63901

Flying Tigers of the 14th
Air Force Assn
P O Box 285
Selden, NY 11784

Intnl B-24 Liberator Club
P O Box 841
San Diego, CA 92112

Tuskegee Airmen, Inc.
5210 Indian Head HWY #1
Oxon Hill, MD 20745

Women Air Force Service Pilots
4300 Caledonia Way
Los Angeles, CA 90065

All Services Associations

Alliance of Women Veterans
P O Box 4881
Los Angeles, CA 90048

American Defense Institute
214 Mass Ave NE #200
Washington, DC 20001

American Gold Star Mothers
2128 Leroy Place NW
Washington, DC 20008

China-Burma-India Assn
PO Box 2665
La Habra, CA 90631

Counterparts(Advisors in VN)
P O Box 40
Circleville, WV 26804

Korean War Ex-POW Assn
4801 Goldfield #163
San Antonio, TX 78218

Korean War Veterans Assn
PO Box 127
Caruthers, CA 93609

Korean War Veterans
Memorial Trust Fund
8656 Park Lane #2008
Dallas, TX 75231

Military Order of Foreign Wars
155 South Main Street
Providence, RI 02903

NAM-POW, Inc.
17159 Tam O'Shanter
Poway, CA 92064

National Assn for Black Veterans
PO BOX 11432
Milwaukee, WI 53211

Uniformed Service Disabled
Retirees
5909 Alta Monte NE
Albuquerque, NM 87110

The Uniformed Services Assn
1304 Vincent Place
McLean, VA 22101

Vietnam Era Vets Assn
242 Prairie Avenue
Providence, RI 02907

The addresses of many reunion associations change periodically with the election of new officers or reunion organizers. To obtain the current address of any of the above reunion organizations or of 8,500 others contact:

Service Reunions
3686 King Street, Suite 172
Alexandria, VA 22303

(703) 845-9838

TO LOCATE FORMER AIR FORCE AND ARMY AIR FORCE PILOT CADETS

Aviation Cadet Alumni Association was formed to provide ex-cadets with current addresses of their former classmates. Former Air Force and Army Air Force Cadets are invited to submit their flying class, primary, basic and advanced schools. Approximately 17,000 names and addresses are now available by flight class to those participants who send a self-addressed stamped envelope to either address below (both maintain identical information):

Harry C. Bradshaw
RFD #1
Newmarket, NH 03857

Robert C. White
54 Seton Trail
Ormond Beach, FL 32704

VETERANS ASSOCIATION FOR SERVICE ACTIVITIES ABROAD

Veterans Association for Service Activities Abroad was organized to locate and assist, if possible, families of former allies who were anxious to be reunited with relatives in the United States. VASAA also has an extensive project to locate all veterans who are members of the Church of Jesus Christ of Latter Day Saints (Mormons). These veterans may have served in any branch of the Armed Forces of their respective countries and during any period of time, whether on active duty or in reserve or National Guard status. It has contacts with many organizations in the United States and foreign countries. Since 1984, VASAA has assisted numerous families to be reunited with relatives, bringing refugees from camps in Southeast Asia or from Viet Nam, Ethiopia, Iran, and Europe through United Nations programs.

VASAA
P.O.Box 17815
Salt Lake City, Utah 84117-0815

(801) 278-7674

HOW TO LOCATE FORMER MILITARY DOCTORS

Two medical directories that list the names and current addresses of physicians are recommended to disabled veterans who are trying to substantiate a claim and need to locate the physicians who treated them for their service-connected disabilities.

They are The Directory of Medicine Specialists, by Marquis Who's Who, and The American Medical Directory, by the American Medical Association.

Both references list a doctor's medical speciality and type of practice. The Directory of Medical Specialists also provides biographical information, such as military service, including a physician's service period, branch of military service, and former rank.

This biographical information can be particularly helpful to disabled veterans who can't remember their doctors' first names. Both directories can usually be found in large public libraries. Another source that disabled veterans might find useful in locating physicians is the American Medical Association's computer data file in Chicago. Veterans can request the address of a physician by writing to:

Data Release
American Medical Association
535 North Dearborn St.
Chicago, IL 60610.

SOMEONE MAY BE LOOKING FOR YOU!

If you are a veteran there is a good chance that someone you served with or your reunion organization is actively seeking you. If you do not belong to a reunion organization or a veterans organization you should consider joining one. These organizations are made up of veterans who have contributed time, money and effort to promote issues that benefit all veterans. By becoming a member of an organization you will make it easier for your unit reunion organizers and others to find you.

CHAPTER SIX

HOW TO OBTAIN MILITARY RECORDS, UNIT AND SHIP ROSTERS, AND ORGANIZATIONAL RECORDS

This chapter describes how you can obtain individual military records, unit records and unit histories. These records are an important source of information in any search of former military member or for a military reunion.

MILITARY RECORDS OF PRESENT, FORMER AND RETIRED MILITARY MEMBERS

Limited information from personnel records is available to anyone. The information which can be provided under the Freedom of Information Act (some of this information pertains to members on active duty or those in the reserves and National Guard) includes: rank/grade; name; duty status; date of rank/grade; service number; dependents (including name, sex and age); gross salary; geographical locations of duty assignments; future assignment (approved); unit or office telephone number; source of commission (officers); military/civilian education level; promotion sequence number; awards and decorations, duty status, official photograph, records of court-martial trials (unless classified), city/town and state of last known residence and the date of that address, place of induction and separation. The place of birth, date of and location of death, and the place of burial of deceased veterans can also be released. Complete personnel and health records are available to former members or their next of kin. Because of the Privacy Act the general public will not be provided with medical information, SSN or present address. To obtain records or particular information send a copy of Standard Form 180 "Request Pertaining to Military Records" (form is at the end of the book). Standard Form 180 is available from most veterans organizations or military installations. You can make a photocopy of the form from the one in this book. Include as much information about the veteran as possible. You must state on Standard Form 180 if you are requesting information under the Freedom of Information Act. There is no charge to former service members or their next of kin; however, others may pay a nominal fee for research and photocopying. Read and prepare the form carefully and mail to the appropriate address on the form. A reply may take from one to six months. The NPRC receives up to 200,000 letters and requests each month.

UNIT AND SHIP'S ROSTERS

Anyone can obtain copies of a unit or ship's rosters (list of personnel) or organizational records by requesting them from the National Personnel Records Center, the National Archives or the appropriate Armed Force. If the roster is needed to support a VA claim, there is usually no cost. You may obtain such records at a minimum cost of $8.30 (deposit) an hour plus a searching cost of $13.25 per hour if your request is for matters other than VA claims. Reunion requests receive low priority and will take more time to process. You may also make a "Freedom of Information Act Request" for a roster and there is no fee charged by the National Personnel Records Center and usually a small fee by the Armed Services.

If you are planning a reunion or need the service number of an individual, a roster is the place to start. The roster will have name, rank and service number (if prior to July 1, 1969 for Army and Air Force, July 1, 1972 for Navy and Marine Corps and October 1, 1974 for Coast Guard) but Social Security numbers will be removed. Be sure to state in your letter the date of the roster requested (e.g., May 1940) and that this is a "Freedom of Information Act Request" (do not mention reunions on this request). The National Personnel Records Center has copies of the following:

1. US Army Morning Reports and Personnel rosters from November 1, 1912 to 1974 and all subsequent reports (including SIDPERS reports) after Morning Reports were discontinued. All rosters for

Army and Army Air Force units for the years 1944, 45 and 46 were destroyed.

2.US Air Force Morning Reports from September 1947 to June 30, 1966 when the Morning Reports were discontinued. The Air Force did not prepare unit rosters.

3.US Navy Muster Rolls from 1939 through 1946.

National Personnel Records Center (314) 263-3901
9700 Page Blvd.
St. Louis, MO 63132-5100

US Navy Muster Rolls from 1947 to the present are available from:

Department of the Navy
Bureau of Naval Personnel
Washington, DC 20370-5000

Lists of ship's crew members may be obtained for periods indicated below.

Navy muster rolls (enlisted only) listed by command from June 1939 to October 1956 are available on microfilm by writing (charge of $7.00-$9.00):

Military Services Branch
Military Archives
National Archives
Washington, D.C. 20408

Deck logs including lists of officers are obtainable from June 1939 to June 1945 from the National Archives at the same address listed above.

US Marine Corps Muster Rolls (unit rosters) and Unit Diaries from January 1, 1956 to the present are available from:

Commandant of the Marine Corps (703) 640-3942
Headquarters USMC/MMRB-106
Records Branch
Building 2008
Quantico, VA 22134-0001

Prior to January 1, 1956 from:

Marine Corps Historical Center   (202) 433-3840
History and Museum Division Bldg 58
Washington Navy Yard
Washington, DC 20347-0580

Muster Rolls (includes officers and enlisted) from Marine Corps units may be obtained by specifying the exact organization and time period. Late 1700's to 1966 rolls are available on microfilm by writing:

Commandant of the Marine Corps
Code HDH-2
Washington, D.C. 20380-0001

US Coast Guard Muster Rolls from 1914 for vessels, districts, life boat stations, miscellaneous units, and recruiting stations. These are available from:

National Archives
and Records Administration
Washington, DC 20408

NOTE: Many of these rosters and lists are taken from microfilm and the quality can be very poor because of age or fire damage. It is advisable to request rosters for several months before and after actual date needed. Unit/ship rosters usually contain the names, rank and service numbers of assigned members.

PARTIAL UNIT ROSTERS

Veterans of the Vietnam War operates a computerized locator service for Vietnam veterans. To register or request a search (individual or unit) send a $1.00 donation. A unit search will list all members who were assigned to a particular unit that is in their computer files:

VVN, Inc.   (800) 843-8626
2090 Bald Mountain Road
Wilkes-Barre, PA 18702-9609.

Seaweeds Ship's History sells histories of all US Navy, US Army Transports, most US Coast Guard and Liberty ships. They have partial crew rosters of the ships. Lists are free with the purchase of a ship's history or $1.00 without an order. Include a self-addressed stamped envelope:

Seaweeds Ship's History   (304) 652-1525
P O Box 92
Sisterville, WV 26175

MILITARY HISTORICAL ORGANIZATIONS

The following military historical organizations can be of great help in providing unit and ship historical information. While most cannot help in searches for individuals, many have names of unit and ship commanders, officers' registers, key personnel and other individuals who have made significant contributions to a unit's or ship's history. These people, if living, may provide the location of the particular person you are seeking.

US Army Center of Military History
20 Massachusetts Avenue NW
Washington, DC 20001
(202) 272-0308 (unit histories)

US Army Military History Institute
Carlisle Barracks, PA 17013

Marine Corps Historical Foundation
Bldg 58 Washington Navy Yard
Washington, DC 20347
(202) 433-3914
(202) 433-3840

Military
(monthly military history newspaper)
2122 28th Street
Sacramento, CA 95818
(916) 457-8990

Command Historian
HQ US Forces Korea/8th US Army
ATTN: SJS Historian
APO San Francisco 96301

Office of Air Force History
AF/CHO, Building 5681
Bolling AFB, DC 20332
(202) 767-5764

15th Air Force Historian
March AFB, CA 92518

Naval Historical Center
Bldg 57 Washington Navy Yard
Washington, DC 20347
(202) 433-4882
(202) 433-2585 (ship's histories)

US Coast Guard Museum
US Coast Guard Academy
New London, CT 06320
(203) 444-8511

HQ, US Air Force Historical
Research Center
USAFHRC/HD
Maxwell AFB, AL 36112
(205) 293-5344

HQ Air Training Command
Historical Office
Randolph AFB, TX 78150-5001
(512) 652-6564

HQ SAC
Historical Office
Offutt AFB, NE 68113-5001
(402) 294-2245

HQ Tactical Air Command
Historical Office
Langley AFB, VA 23665-5001
(804) 764-3186

National Archives and
Records Administration
Washington, DC 20408
(202) 501-5402

US Air Force Museum
P O Box 1903
Wright-Patterson AFB, OH 45433
(513) 255-3284

US Coast Guard Museum NW
1519 Alaskan Way South
Seattle, WA 98134
(206) 286-9608

The Air Force Museum in addition to providing unit histories also publishes "Friends Bulletin" which will list Army Air Force and Air Force reunion notices.

US Military Museums, Historic Sites and Exhibits by Bruce D. Thompson and published by Military Living is one of the most comprehensive books available on this subject. It includes listings of Army, Navy, Air Force, Marine Corps, Coast Guard and NOAA museums in the United States and overseas. It also lists all American military cemeteries and military sites in the National Park System. This 300 page book is a must for people doing military research, reunion planning or who have an interest in our country's military history.

ARMY AND AIR FORCE UNIT HISTORIES

James T. Controvich assist unit historians and associations in preparing and locating unit histories. He also prepares bibliographies for Army and Air Force units. His unit history library consists of over 3,000 volumes. He also has access to many official Army libraries. For additional information contact:

James T. Controvich   (413) 734-4856
97 Mayfield St.
Springfield, MA 01108

RECORDS OF CIVIL SERVICE PERSONNEL AND MILITARY DEPENDENTS

The following information may be obtained under the Freedom of Information Act from records of most present and former federal employees:

1.Name
2.Present and past position titles and occupationalseries
3.Present and past grades
4.Present and past annual salary rates
5. Present and past duty stations
6.Position descriptions

To obtain personnel records of individuals who were employed by the Federal Civil Service, US Postal Service and medical records of dependents of active duty (Army and Air Force) and retired military personnel contact:

National Personnel Records Center   (314) 425-5761
Civilian Personnel Records
111 Winnebago Street
St. Louis, MO 63118

Medical records of Navy, Marine Corps and Coast Guard dependents are located at:

National Personnel Records Center   (314) 263-3901
9700 Page Blvd.
St. Louis, MO 63132-5100

Requests involving retirement, insurance information or medical records of Civil Service personnel should be sent to:

Office of Personnel Management
Compensation Group
1900 E. Street NW
Washington DC 20415

TO ACQUIRE RECORDS RAPIDLY

If you need to obtain records from the National Personnel Records Center in the shortest time possible contact Military Information Enterprises. They employ a retired member of the NPRC who can locate and obtain copies of all records available from the NPRC. Copies of discharge, personnel and medical records, unit rosters and morning reports and organizational records can be secure in two to three weeks. All request are hand carried to the NPRC and are not sent through the mail room. Records can be obtained for individuals, lawyers, investigators, reunion associations and others. For additional information contact:

Military Information Enterprises
Post Office Box 340081
Fort Sam Houston, TX 78234

CHAPTER SEVEN

HOW TO LOCATE ANYONE (CIVILIAN OR MILITARY)

This chapter provides numerous ways to locate anyone whether civilian or military. It explains how federal, state and local government agencies may provide assistance. The same is true of publications and private organizations.

SOCIAL SECURITY ADMINISTRATION

The Social Security Administration (SSA) will forward some unsealed letters to people whose names are listed in their files for certain humanitarian reasons that will be beneficial to the receiver. These reasons vary from locating missing relatives, medical reasons, locating heirs to estates and assisting people with claims, etc. Letters that are accepted will be forwarded to their employers or directly to the individual if he is drawing Social Security benefits.

Before offering assistance, the SSA must determine that it is reasonable to assume the person to be contacted would want to receive the letter and want to reply.

If the person to be contacted is not a beneficiary/recipient (no current address available), the SSA may offer to forward a letter through the last known employer.

The SSA will not offer to forward any correspondence unless the following conditions are met:

1. Strong compelling reasons exist, e.g.,
    a. A strong humanitarian purpose will be served (e.g., a close relative is seriously ill, is dying, or has died).
    b. A minor child is left without parental guidance.
    c. A defendant in a felony case is seeking a defense witness.
    d. A parent wishes to locate a son or daughter.

e. Consent of the missing person is needed in connection with an adoption proceeding for his/her child.

2.The missing person would want to know the contents of the letter.

3.The missing person's disappearance occurred far enough in the past that SSA could reasonably expect to have a usable mailing address.

4.All other possibilities for contacting the missing person have been exhausted.

Forwarding Procedures

1. You must submit your request in writing to the servicing SSA office, giving the following information:

a. Missing person's name and Social Security number.

b. If SSN is unknown, give date and place of birth, name of parents, name and address of last known employer and period of employment.

c. Reason for wanting to contact the person.

d. Last time seen.

e. Other contacts that have been exhausted.

2.Enclose your letter to be forwarded in an unsealed stamped envelope.

Monetary Consideration Involved

A strong compelling reason may be deemed to exist if a monetary or other consideration is involved and it is reasonable to assume that the missing person does not know it. For example:

1.Missing person is a beneficiary of an estate.

2.Insurance proceeds are due the missig person.

3.An important document is being held. (SSA will not forward the document)

The procedures are the same as above except include a personal check, cashier's check, or money order payable to the Social Security Administration in the amount of $3.00 per letter. See your telephone book foi address and telephone number of your local SSA office or call 1-800-234-5772.

INTERNAL REVENUE SERVICE

The Internal Revenue Service (IRS) will forward letters to people in their files that they can identify (with Social Security number) for humane reasons. Such cases are:

1. Urgent or compelling nature, such as a serious illness.
2. Imminent death or death of a close relative.
3. A person seeking a missing relative.

A reunion or tracing a family tree does not qualify as a humane purpose. The IRS will not forward letters concerning debts. If a letter is forwarded by the IRS and is undeliverable by the post office and returned to the IRS, it will be destroyed and the sender will not be notified.

If an address can be found, the letter will be placed in an IRS envelope and the addressee will be advised that the letter is being forwarded in accordance with current IRS policy. The IRS will not divulge the recipient's current address, nor any tax information, and the decision to reply is entirely up to the recipient.

THE TELEPHONE COMPANY

Contact your local telephone company and ask them if they have copies of telephone books of out of town cities, especially if the local library does not have the one you need. Keep in mind that the information operator can give you valuable data in addition to telephone numbers. You can request the information operator to check the entire area code for the person you are seeking. You can get addresses or you can find out if a certain person has a telephone even if it is unlisted in some areas. If you find out the person you are looking for does have an unlisted number, call the operator and have her call the person and ask them to contact you. This service is done only in some areas for emergencies or important matters, so inform the operator of it's importance.

Computer owners who subscribe to Compuserve can use the telephone directory service but must search each name by state.

It is important to point out that military bases have their own telephone system which are completely independent of the civilian (Bell, GTE, etc.) companies. They have their own information operators (see the Base/Post Locator section in chapter two for a list of telephone numbers of these operations).

COLLEGES, UNIVERSITIES, AND ALUMNI ASSOCIATIONS

The Family and Educational Rights and Privacy Act allows schools to release "directory information" to the public without the consent of the student. A student may request that all or part of this information be withheld from the public by making a written request to do so. "Directory Information" includes, but is not limited to, student's name, current address, telephone listing, major, date and place of birth, dates of attendance, degrees and awards received, previous educational agencies or institutions attended.

Many active duty military personnel attend colleges and universities on or near their military installations. A large number of former members of the military (veterans and retired) attend college after their release from the Armed Forces (most use VA educational benefits). Many military members may have attended some institute of higher learning prior to entering the service. Colleges and alumni associations try to keep current addresses of former students and most will either provide the address or will forward a letter. Check with college registrars, main and college libraries to obtain addresses and disclosure policies.

CHURCHES

Churches can be of great assistance in many searches. Most priests, ministers and rabbis know the addresses of their current and former members. Most churches and synagogues maintain records of baptisms, confirmations, first communions, bar mitzvahs, weddings and burials. If you know the religious affiliation of the person you are seeking, this can be a valuable place to obtain addresses and information (e.g., date of birth, former address, names and addresses of friends and relatives).

THE COURT HOUSE AND CITY HALL

Government records such as deeds to property, automobile registration, marriage license, business names, voter registration, professional licenses, tax records, record of trials (civil or criminal) can be a source of information that can give you current addresses and possibly a SSN of people you are searching for. Military people often buy real estate near the bases where they are stationed. As they move, they usually rent the property and the tax bill is mailed to them. This information is public record. Check both the courthouse and city hall for tax and deed information. This is best achieved by mail, in person or through computerized search services. In many areas utility users (water, gas, electricity, cable television) addresses are available, if requested.

Most employees in local government offices can be very helpful especially if you tell them the urgency and reason for your search.

A trip to your local library can help you to identify county and civil jurisdictions as well as their addresses. This information is also available in the National ZIP Code Directory published by the US Postal Service.

THE UNITED STATES POST OFFICE

If you know the former address of the person you are looking for, you may find their current address from the post office. Go to any post office, but preferably to the one they received their mail from and ask for a "Freedom of Information" request form. Or write a letter and request the address under the Freedom of Information Act (you must include their previous address).

The post office will mail you the individual's new address if a change of address has been submitted and it is not over 18 months old (the post office forwards mail for 12 months but keeps this information for 18 months). The cost of this service is only $1.00 and well worth the time and cost involved. If the person has a post office box they will not give you their home address if the box is for personal use, but will give it to law enforcement officials and individuals by court order. If the box is for business use, the post office will give you the name, address and telephone number of the renter.

You may also mail a letter to the person you are seeking at his last known address and if you write on the lower edge of the envelope or below the return address "ADDRESS CORRECTION REQUESTED," the post office will send you a copy of the Change of Address Card or a photocopy of your letter with the forwarding address on it and they will return your letter to you. You may also put "DO NOT FORWARD" and the letter will be returned to you and they will provide you with the individual's new address. The 18 month rule applies here. There is a fee of thirty five cents for this service. You might want to use this method when you forward letters through the World–Wide Locators, Base Locators, Alumni Associations and Social Security Administration and you may find the person's current address in this manner.

Write the Postmaster (especially smaller towns) of the town where the person once lived. You will possibly get some useful information and assistance. Many small town postmasters have held their job for 30 to 40 years and know the location of numerous people who once lived there.

THE LIBRARY

If recommended means have failed to locate the person you are searching, spend some time in your local library. The information section of most libraries has telephone books from numerous cities, telephone directories on microfiche of all major areas, crisscross city directories, reference books of local areas, directories of national telephone numbers, and much more. Talk to the librarians and tell them what you are doing, and you may get some help and ideas. The city directory is one of the most important search tools available. Most main libraries keep old editions and these can provide the former address of an individual. Some main libraries will look up listings for you over the telephone.

The History and Genealogy section of the library have rosters of people who belonged to military and veterans organizations or you may want to search based upon location, events, etc. The opportunities are endless.

The Church of Jesus Christ of Latter-day Saints (Mormons) has the largest family history (genealogical) library in the world and numerous local family history libraries. The libraries contain large amounts of genealogical information including the Social Security Death Index, Military Casualties and POW files and numerous telephone books on microfiche. For further information contact your local family history library:

Church of Jesus Christ of Latter-day Saints
Family History Department
35 North West Temple
Salt Lake City, Utah 84150

If you have the opportunity to visit the Library of Congress, there are literally millions of books and reference materials that can be of help to you. Particularly helpful are the registers that individual military services once published that list all Warrant Offices and Officers. Some military and public libraries have copies of Officers Registers. Some of the last issues have the name and Social Security number included (for active duty and retired). This practice was discontinued in 1976. Earlier editions have name and service number listed along with military service information. They were usually published annually or biennial.

Most military installations have base libraries and museums. Many have some information about the units that were stationed there. Call the information operator of the base concerned to obtain the telephone number of the base library and museum. Remember to ask for help from the library staff. They can be of great assistance to you in your search.

LOCATING MISSING PEOPLE THROUGH PRIVATE INVESTIGATORS

Some difficult cases may need the help of a professional investigator. There are numerous investigators listed in local telephone books, but before you enter into any agreement, check their references and costs closely. One agency that has an impeccable reputation with outstanding results in handling extremely difficult cases is the Family Search Service. This agency charges reasonable rates for searches that are successful. You may contact them at the following address:

Family Search Service   (216) 251-8642
10802 St. Mark Avenue
Cleveland, OH 44111

National Association of Investigative Specialists (NAIS) is a national network of private investigative professionals and/or agencies who are specialists in some aspect of the investigative industry. The organization has over 1500 members. For a recommendation for your particular needs, contact:

National Association of   (512) 832-9376
Investigative Specialists
PO Box 33244
Austin, TX 78764

Charles Eric Gordon is an attorney concentrating on locating persons who have been missing for a substantial period of time or about whom little information is known. A consultant to law firms, corporations, government agencies and even to foreign governments in tracing missing witnesses, heirs, beneficiaries, relatives, debtors and others, attorney Gordon will also counsel individuals with regard to difficult or unusual cases. With his worldwide contacts and many years of experience as both an attorney and an investigator, Gordon also assists in obtaining information and public records which, although technically available to the public, are actually very difficult to access: e.g., vital records, voter registration and court records (where legally available) and even copies of baptismal, cemetery and property records, some of which may be over a hundred years old. Although Gordon's fees, in the range of $100.00 to $125.00 per hour are admittedly in the high range, where other sources or attempts have failed, or where time is of the essence, such an expenditure can prove well worth it. This is especially true with cases involving persons who were last known to be out of the United States. Contact him at the following address:

Charles Eric Gordon, Esq.   (718) 793-3750
118-11 Queens Boulevard
Forest Hills, New York 11375

NEWSPAPERS AND MAGAZINES

There are several periodicals devoted to locating missing people that are of value. When seeking military or former military people, we recommend the following weekly newspapers: *Army Times, Navy Times, Air Force Times and Federal Times*. These are the most popular and most widely read newspapers of the Armed Services and Civil Service personnel. Federal Times is read primarily by present and former Civil Servants, a large portion of whom are military veterans, retired military or members of the Reserve Components. These newspapers have locator columns that may help you. Readers include current military members, but also many reserve, National Guard, retired and former members. You will probably get a response to any published assistance you request. Following is the address for all the newspapers:

Army Times Publishing Co.
6883 Commercial Drive   (800) 424-9335
Springfield, VA 22159

The largest veteran oriented newspaper is Stars and Stripes: The National Herald. When seeking a veteran or publicizing a reunion this publication should be considered.

Stars and Stripes: (202) 829-3225
The National Herald
278 Carrol ST NE
Washington, DC 20012

Also an effective newspaper is the one sold in the last known location where the person you are seeking lived. Place an advertisement in the personal section. Thousands of people read the classified section and you may get a response. Write an advertisement similar to the following:

Chief Master Sgt. Joe L. James
Urgent, Anyone who knows his
whereabouts call collect (513) 888-8888

A letter to the editor of a small town newspaper will usually bring you some help in your search. Your local library can give you names and addresses of newspapers that you will need to contact, for Gale's Directory of Publications.

People Searching News

People Searching News is an excellent six issue subscription magazine with emphasis on adoption and missing person searches. ($16.50) PSN also operates a 24 hour a day no-fee Assistance Referral Hotline (305) 370-7100. They can offer you the services of more than 2800 researchers. Fees are minimal. PSN has a classified advertisement section and subscribers will research local telephone and city directories, if requested. For additional information and an "Introductory Packet" send a legal size self-addressed stamped envelope (with 52 cents postage) to:

People Searching News
P O Box 22611
Ft. Lauderdale, FL 33335-2611

THE RESEARCHER CLEARINGHOUSE

The Researchers Clearinghouse networks with more than 2,800 genealogists, post adoption researchers and private investigators throughout the United States and in some foreign countries. Search services are available to the public through TRC at local and national levels at reduced fees. For a general list of services send a long SASE to:

TRC
P.O. Box 22363
Fort Lauderdale, FL 33335-2363.

Lifeline: The Action Guide to Adoption Search

This publication is the most valuable guide available in conducting an successful adoption search. It is a unique resource for all adoptees, birthparents and adoptive parents. It contains 409 pages of the latest search techniques along with 59 sample letters, documents and checklists covering all 50 states and 14 countries. This book gives a detailed 21 point directory of vital search resources for every state; including current laws, records data/costs, inside tips and instruction from local search experts and much more. It includes over 1,000 updated names, addresses, and telephone numbers of public and private organizations used daily by searchers.

Reunions, the magazine

Reunions, the magazine, a new quarterly, is the only publication concentrating exclusively on reunions including military reunions. *Reunions, the magazine,* regularly offers tips, leads and hints to help with your search. The column, Military Stars, discusses the fine points of military reunion planning. Reunion Reveille is a list of upcoming military reunions. Other regular columns, departments, and feature articles provide guidance for location of individuals, encouragement, and advice for your search. Special features are planned to commemorate reunions celebrating significant upcoming military anniversaries. Available by subscription: one year $22; two years $40 if you enclose payment ($24/year or $48/2 years, if billed). Make checks payable to Reunions, the magazine and mail to :

Reunions, the magazine
PO Box 11727
Milwaukee, WI 53211-0727

TO LOCATE PILOTS WHO ARE LICENSED BY THE FAA

The Federal Aviation Agency (FAA) will provide the address and certification of a licensed pilot if you provide the name and date of birth. You can also use a SSN or a certification number. If the name is unique they can provide an address without these identifying items. Write to:

FAA Airmen Certification Branch
VN-460
P O Box 25082
Oklahoma City, OK 73125

TO LOCATE PEOPLE THROUGH THE SALVATION ARMY

The Salvation Army conducts searches of missing people for immediate family members only through their national missing person network. Contact your local Salvation Army Social Service Center for information and a registration form. There is a $10.00 fee for this service.

TO LOCATE PEOPLE WHO ARE DUE UNCLAIMED ASSETS

There are numerous companies who search for people who are heirs or are eligible to receive unclaimed assets held by state governments. These companies require a portion of all monies that are received by the persons they locate. Since they are profit motivated you may wish to contact one if unclaimed assets are involved. Here is the name and address of one of the larger companies that deal in unclaimed assets:

Capital Tracers, Inc.   (800) 321-9192
207 West 25th Street
New York, NY 10001

TO LOCATE MILITARY DEPENDENTS WHO ATTENDED OVERSEAS HIGH SCHOOLS (AND TEACHERS)

Sometimes the best way to contact or locate an individual is by first locating their children. Overseas Brats is a non-profit organization of overseas high school alumni comprised of former dependents of US military, government and civilian personnel. It provides free information to all inquires concerning over 187 alumni groups of 130 high schools in 46 countries.

Overseas Brats   (512) 349-1394
P O Box 29805 DJ
San Antonio, TX 78229

OSCAR is a database that can supply limited information about former military dependents who attended overseas schools. You may reach OSCAR at the following address:

Overseas Schools Combined Alumni Registry
P O Box 7763   (202) 362-4203
Washington, DC 20044
Send self-addressed stamped envelope.

The American Overseas Schools Archives maintains memorabilia pertaining to all aspects of kindergarten through twelfth grade education of American children abroad. The Archives has yearbooks, scrapbooks, curricula, newspaper, magazine and journal articles, photographs, official papers and documents, personal histories and memoirs of all kinds. Contact:

American Overseas Schools Archives   (602) 523-4203
University of Northern Arizona
Box 5774
Flagstaff, AZ 86011

Information concerning retired Department of Defense School teachers may be obtained from:

DODS Retirement Group
NBG Dist. Superintendents Office
Box 2326
APO New York, NY 09696-0005

TO LOCATE PEOPLE
TRAVELING OVERSEAS

To locate US citizens traveling abroad call the State Department's Citizens Emergency Center: (202) 647-5225.

CONGRESSIONAL ASSISTANCE

If you are not getting results or answers from federal agencies or the military, you can write your United States Congressman or Senator and ask for their assistance. The military and other government agencies are very responsive to inquiries from Members of Congress. You can expect a quick reply to your letter, usually within two weeks.

Include all the information you can about the person you are trying to locate, why you need to contact him, what steps you have taken so far and the results of these steps.

To write your Congressman in the House of Representatives, the address is:

Honorable John Doe
United States House of Representatives
Washington, DC 20515

To write your Senator the address is:

Honorable John Doe
United States Senate
Washington, DC 20510

See your local telephone book for your Congressman's name and telephone number. It may help, if you call his office first and talk to the administrative assistant about your circumstance.

THE NATIONWIDE LOCATOR

The Nationwide Locator provides numerous computer search services to facilitate locating missing people, both military and civilian, such as:

Social Security number search: provide a SSN and you will receive last reported address of the individual you are seeking ($30.00).

National Criss-Cross search: provide an old mailing address (street and number, city, state and ZIP) and get the current reported address ($30.00).

National Surname Search provides address and listed telephone numbers of any of 91 million people nationwide. Provide a name and you will receive names, addresses, and listed telephone numbers of everyone in the country with that name ($25.00).

Other programs include drivers license searches, national change of address, license plate search.

The Nationwide Locator has special prices for reunions and other large numbers of names. Prices are as low as $3.00 per name.

For brochure write:

The Nationwide Locator
Post Office Box 39903
San Antonio, TX 78218

The Nationwide Locator is owned by Military Information Enterprises and is member of the San Antonio Retail Merchants Association.

PERSONAL SEARCH BY THE AUTHOR

The author conducts searches for missing people with a military connection. He has very high success rates for his searches. For information write:

Lt. Col. Richard S. Johnson
Military Information Enterprises
Post Office Box 340081
Fort Sam Houston, TX 78234

CHAPTER EIGHT

HOW TO LOCATE PEOPLE FOR A MILITARY REUNION

This chapter provides recommended steps for a reunion organizer to take to locate former members of a military unit for a reunion.

STEPS TO TAKE TO LOCATE FORMER MEMBERS OF A UNIT FOR A REUNION

1. OBTAIN A COPY OF THE UNIT ROSTER FOR THE PERIOD OF THE REUNION:
   a. Request roster from the NPRC or the appropriate Armed Force.
   b. Obtain a partial roster, if available.
   c. Write historical organizations for unit histories, names and addresses of ship or unit commanders or other key personnel. Write them and ask for copies of unit rosters, unit orders, etc.
   d. Write other reunion organizations and appropriate veterans organizations for unit historical information, copies of rosters and name and addresses of former members of your unit.
   e. Establish a network. Get your entire membership involved in locating ther members they may have had contact with. Get old addresses, copies of unit orders, etc. Check officers registers for services numbers, SSN and dates of birth.
2. ESTABLISH A DATA BASE ON A COMPUTER:
   a. Record all the names from the rosters, unit orders, individual input, unit histories on a card file or a computer file. List name, rank, service number, Social Security number, VA Claim number, current address and telephone number, old address if current one is unknown, and date of death if deceased.

3. PUBLISH A NEWS RELEASE:
   a. Send to all veterans magazines, newspapers, newsletters and organizations. Send to all major daily newspapers. Use Military Reunion News reunion announcement program.
   b. Register your reunion with:
      1. Service Reunions
      2. Armed Forces Reunion BBS
      3. Office of the Secretary of the Army (Army and Army Air Force Units)
      4. The American Legion's VetNet
4. SEND LETTERS TO MISSING MEMBERS FROM UPDATED ROSTER THROUGH:
   a. VA
   b. Service locators (active and, reserved, National Guard, retired)
   c. All veterans organizations, unit reunion associations and specialized organizations etc.
5. SEND UPDATED UNIT ROSTER TO VETERANS LOCATORS:
   a. Use disk to disk if possible.
     (3.5 or 5.25)
6. WRITE:
   a. Mayors
   b. Postmasters
   c. Newspaper Editors
7. SEND ALL MISSING NAMES AND FORMER ADDRESSES OR SSN TO THE NATIONWIDE LOCATOR:
   a. Use disk to disk if possible.
8. CLEAN-UP REMAINING MISSING ADDRESSES MANUALLY WITH:
   a. City directories
   b. Telephone books
   c. Civilian locators at military bases
   d. Alumni associations
   e. Officers Register

MILITARY UNIT REUNIONS

Numerous unit reunions are held annually. If you want to find out when and where these reunions are held, the major veteran organizations magazines have columns that publish notices of reunions. The DAV, The

American Legion, VFW magazines are good examples. Most public libraries have copies. You can contact local chapters or the national headquarters of these organizations for copies of their magazines. Veterans Administration offices also have copies available. Reunion organizations can be an excellent sources for locating veterans, if you know their former unit.

You can also contact the following addresses to register or to find out if a particular unit has an association.

ARMY UNIT REUNIONS
Office of the Secretary of the Army   (703) 614-0739
Public Affairs Office
ATTN: Community Relations Division
Pentagon, Room 2E631
Washington, DC 20310

This office maintains a free roster of Associations of Army organizations. It is rather large and contains addresses, telephone numbers and contact persons for several hundred associations and organizations. If you are a member of an Army association, be sure it is listed with this office.

ALL ARMED FORCES REUNIONS

The Armed Forces Reunion BBS has an electronic bulletin board for the listing and accessing of Armed Forces reunions. It is available to all active duty personnel and veterans. All that is required is a computer, a modem and telephone line access. The Armed Forces Reunion BBS originally listed US Coast Guard reunions, but it has been expanded to include all Uniformed Services. The sponsor is the Armed Forces Reunion BBS, a group of Coast Guardsmen who served on the Merrill during World War II. It has over 3,000 permanent reunion groups listed in its data base. There is no charge to access the data base. Send a large self-addressed stamped envelope with written request for a manual search or to manually post a reunion. (Small donation is appreciated.)

Armed Forces Reunion BBS
P O Box 681
Enka, NC 28728-0681

FOR COMPUTER USERS

To access and scan data base dial:

(704) 667-8021
300/1200/2400/9600 BAUD RATES SUPPORTED
8-N-1 On line 24 hours a day.

THE AMERICAN LEGION MAGAZINE'S TELEPHONE REUNION INFORMATION SYSTEM (VETNET)

The American Legion Magazine has created a 24 hour a day telephone and computer service to provide information about military reunions. Dial 1-800-348-VETS and ask for the five digit vet group number of the particular units you are searching for. Then dial 1-900-773-VETS from a touch tone phone and when asked enter the VetNet number of the unit which you want information. This call cost $1.00 per minute. You will hear a recorded message from the unit coordinator about their planned reunion. After the message is completed you will be asked if you want to use the units MailCall feature to leave a message. The American Legion Magazine is attempting to enroll 10,000 reunion organizations into VetNet. For free registration write:

VetNet
PO Box 1055
Indianapolis, IN 46206

PLANNING A MILITARY REUNION

If you are considering holding a reunion, or you are the next reunion chair-person, then it is strongly recommended that you contact Bill Masciangelo, USMC (Ret.), the creator of the ITT Sheraton Military/Veterans Network. Bill is a reunion planning expert and has written extensively on the subject of military reunion planning. His work has appeared in Leatherneck Magazine, Military Reunion News, and Reunions, The Magazine. He is the co-author of the recently published Military Reunion Handbook: A Guide for Reunion Planners. As a direct result of the increased interest in military reunions and the planning of these emotional and important events, Bill has conducted training workshops across the country. As of this year, over 600 military reunion planners have attended his one day conferences, are free for the volunteer reunion planner. Everything from hotel negotiations, finding people, to food and beverage planning considerations are discussed. Small break-out groups meet during the morning to allow reunion planners to meet and discuss important topic issues. Ten key topics are introduced to the planners. The reunion planning conferences are only one of the many services that Bill continues to offer. He is available to assist with the planning of your reunion at no cost to your organization. Also, Bill can be a consultant, meeting with your site selection committee or board members and providing services to guide you through the reunion planning specifically, have become very sophisticated and complex. There is now a growing need for professional assistance. Reunion planners can no longer afford to leave this planning process to luck and the "We have always done it that way" way of thinking. You may contact Bill Masciangelo at:

Bill Masciangelo   (703) 845-9838
3686 King Street
Box 172
Alexandria, VA 22302

Military Reunion News

Military Reunion News publishes two items of interest to reunion planners. A bimonthly newsletter, The Military Reunion Newsletter, and a CO-OP MAIL PROGRAM of news releases publicizing reunion notices.

The Newsletter contains "how to" information on planning and executing a reunion along with ideas and hints to make your reunion memorable. Some aspect of reunion planning is featured in each issue's cover story. Topics covered have included, finding your lost unit members, cruising as an alternative reunion site, and negotiating with hotels. The annual subscription fee is $15.00.

The CO-OP MAIL PROGRAM combines your reunion announcement with several others in News Release format which is then distributed to almost 1,980 publications and outlets for $69.50. Releases are distributed through Service Reunions, the Armed Forces Reunion BBS, and to the following outlets:

Military /Veteran association periodicals civilian newspapers (dailies and weeklies), military base newspapers, public libraries, VA hospitals, and state and county veteran service officers.

A special $80.00 offer of one monthly CO-OP mailing and annual subscription to the Newsletter is available.

Military Reunion News   (512) 438-4177
P O Box 355
Bulverde, TX 78163

Military Reunion Handbook

Military Reunion Handbook A Guide For Reunion Planners is a step by step manual for reunion organizers that deals with every aspect of military reunions. This 214 page book was written by Bill Masciangelo and Tom Ninkovich who are the two most knowledgeable people in the country on planning and conducting a reunion. This book is an absolute must for every reunion association whether they are planning their first or fiftieth reunion.

SERVICE REUNIONS NATIONAL REGISTRY

This is a database of over 8,200 military reunions held throughout the country. Service Reunions continues to be indispensable to anyone wishing to publicize their military reunion and provides a source of information for individuals looking for a reunion.

Service Reunions has been instrumental in reuniting thousands of vets looking for their old units or ships.

To register your reunion notice and have it listed one time, in several civilian newspapers across the country, complete the following form and return it with a $3.00 donation to help defray the cost of this special notification. (If you only wish to keep your organization's information updated in the registry, complete the form and return it at no charge.)

To search for a military reunion, complete your service and unit/ship information on the form on the next page and return with a self-addressed stamped envelope and a $1.00 donation to:

Service Reunions   (703) 845-9838
3686 King Street, Suite 172
Alexandria, VA 22302

REGISTRATION FORM

Service _____

Unit (Be very specific) _____

_____

Period: WW II   Korea   Vietnam   Beirut _____

_____ Grenada   Panama   Desert Stm   Other _____

Reunion Dates: _____
             Month   Days   Year

Where: _____
       City   State   Hotel

Contact: _____
    First Name   Last Name

Address _____

_____
    City   State   ZIP plus 4

Phone: (___) _____

Estimated Attendance at

last/next reunion: _____ National/Regional Reunion ___

Frequency: _____Annual_____Biennial

REUNIONS FOR DESERT STORM, GRENADA AND PANAMA

If you were involved in these military activities or have friends or relatives that were involved in these military activities, preparation for a future military reunion should be done now.

The following recommendations should be accomplished now:

1. Appoint one or more people who were in the units involved to be reunion coordinators.
2 Collect rosters of the unit that include names, ranks and Social Security numbers of the members.
3. Obtain home addresses of all unit members.
4. Place all information in a computer database.
5. Keep in touch with all original unit members by letter or a newsletter at least once a year.
6. Prepare for your reunion now. Select a sight and date. Inform all members.
7. Seek donations from unit members to defray organizational and mailing cost.
8. Register your reunion organization as soon as possible with:
   a. Service Reunions
   b. Armed Forces Reunion BBS
   c. Secretary of the Army
   d. The American Legion's VetNet
9. Subscribe to Military Reunion News
10. Purchase copies of *The Military Reunion Handbook* for all key reunion planners.

If the above recommendations are done now it will be easier to locate all former members of a unit. All future reunions will be easier to conduct and will have a greater participation.

CHAPTER NINE

HOW TO LOCATE PEOPLE THROUGH STATE GOVERNMENT RECORDS

This chapter provides information on how to obtain addresses of individuals through vital statistics, motor vehicle registrations and drivers license offices of the various states.

LOCATE BY DRIVER'S LICENSE, MOTOR VEHICLE REGISTRATION

Most people have a driver's license and own a car. You can obtain their address by contacting the driver's license and/or motor vehicle department of the issuing state. Each charge a fee, usually two to five dollars. Most active duty military personnel keep their driver's license and their cars registered in their home state when they are stationed within the United States. When they are transferred overseas they usually must get a new driver's license and vehicle tags issued by the US military or from the country where they are stationed.

STATE DRIVERS LICENSE OFFICES

To obtain a persons address or driving record write to the appropriate state office below. (A few states will not provide an address without permission of the individual.) Please write for information and fees charged for this service.

ALABAMA
Drivers License Division
Certificate Section
P O Box 1471
Montgomery, AL 36192

ALASKA
Department of Public Safety
Drivers License Safety
Pouch N
Juneau, AK 99801

ARIZONA
Motor Vehicle Division
1801 West Jefferson Street
Phoenix, AZ 85007

ARKANSAS
Office of Drivers Services
Traffic Violation Rpt Unit
P O Box 1272
Little Rock, AR 72203

CALIFORNIA
Dept of Motor Vehicles
P O Box 944247
Sacramento, CA 94244-2470

COLORADO
Traffic Records Section
140 West 6th Avenue
Room 103
Denver, CO 80204

CONNECTICUT
Dept of Motor Vehicles
Copy Record Section
60 State Street
Wethersfield, CT 06109

DELAWARE
Department of Public Safety
Motor Vehicles Division
P O Box 698
Dover, DE 19901

DISTRICT OF COLUMBIA
Bureau of Motor Vehicle Svc
301 C. Street N.W.
Washington, DC 20001

FLORIDA
Dept of Highway Safety
Drivers License Div,
Kirkhaam Bldg
Tallahassee, FL 32301

GEORGIA
Department of Public Safety
Drivers Service Section
P O Box 1456
Atlanta, GA 30371

HAWAII
Violations Bureau
824 Bethel
Honolulu, HI 96813

IDAHO
Department of Law Enforcement
Motor Vehicle Division
P O Box 55
Boise, ID 83707

ILLINOIS
Secretary of State
Drivers Services Section
2701 South Dirksen Parkway
Springfield, IL 62723

INDIANA
Bureau of Motor Vehicles
Drivers License Records
100 N. Senate Avenue
State Office Building
Indianapolis, IN 46204

IOWA
Department of Transportation
Office of Driver's Services
Park Fair Mall
100 Euclid Avenue
P.O. Box 9204
Des Moines, IA 50306-9204

KANSAS
Division of Vehicles
Driver Control Bureau
State Office Building
Topeka, KS 66626

KENTUCKY
Division of Driver Licenses
State Office Building
Frankfort, KY 40622

LOUISIANA
Department of Public Safety
Office of Motor Vehicles
Box 64886
Baton Rouge, LA 70896

MAINE
Department of State
Motor Vehicle Division
State House Station 29
Augusta, ME 04333

MARYLAND
Motor Vehicle Administration
6601 Ritchie Highway N.E.
Glen Burnie, MD 21062

MASSACHUSETTS
Registry of Motor Vehicles
100 Nashua Street
Boston, MA 02114

MICHIGAN
Department of State
Bureau of Driver & Vehicle Srv.
7064 Crowner Driver
Lansing, MI 49818

MINNESOTA
Department of Public Safety
Drivers License Division
Room 108 State Highway Bld.
St. Paul, MN 55155

MISSISSIPPI
Mississippi Highway Safety Patrol
Drivers License Division
P O Box 958
Jackson, MS 39205

MISSOURI
Bureau of Driver Licenses
P O Box 200
Department of Revenue
Jefferson City, MO 65101

MONTANA
Montana Highway Patrol
303 N Roberts
Helena, MT 59620

NEBRASKA
Department of Motor Vehicles
Driver Records Section
P O Box 94789
Lincoln, NE 68509

NEVADA
Department of Motor Vehicles
Drivers License Division
Carson City, NV 89711

NEW HAMPSHIRE
Division of Motor Vehicles
Drivers License Division
J H Hayes Building
Concord, NH 03305

NEW JERSEY
Dept of Law and Public Safety
Drivers License Division
P O Box 7068
West Trenton, NJ 08628

NEW MEXICO
Motor Vehicle Division
Driver Services Bureau
P O Box 1028
Santa Fe, NM 87504

NEW YORK
Department of Motor Vehicles
Empire State Plaza
Albany, NY 12228

NORTH CAROLINA
Traffic Records Section
Division of Motor Vehicles
1100 New Bern Avenue
Raleigh, NC 27697

NORTH DAKOTA
Drivers License Department
Capitol Grounds
Bismark, ND 58505

OHIO
Bureau of Motor Vehicles
P O Box 16520
Columbus, OH 43216

OKLAHOMA
Driver Records Service
Department of Public Safety
P O Box 11415
Oklahoma City, OK 73136

OREGON
Motor Vehicle Division
1905 Lona Avenue, N.E.
Salem, OR 97314

PENNSYLVANIA
Department of Transportation
Bureau of Drivers Licensing
Rm 212, Transp & Sfty Bldg
Harrisburg, PA 17120

RHODE ISLAND
Registry of Motor Vehicles
Room 101 G
State Office Bldg
Providence, RI 02903

SOUTH CAROLINA
Department of Highways and
Public Transportation
Drivers Records Clerk, Section 201
P O Box 1498
Columbia, SC 29216

SOUTH DAKOTA
Department of Commerce
and Regulation
118 West Capitol
Pierre, SD 57501

TENNESSEE
Department of Safety
Jackson Building
Nashville, TN 37219

TEXAS
Driver Records Division
40th and Jackson Avenue
Austin, TX 78779

UTAH
Drivers License Division
314 State Office Building
Salt Lake City, UT 84114

VERMONT
Department of Motor Vehicles
120 State Street
Montpelier, VT 05602

VIRGINIA
Department of Motor Vehicles
Driver Licensing and Information
P O Box 27412
Richmond, VA 23269

WASHINGTON
Department of Licensing
P O Box 9909
Olympia, WA 98504

WEST VIRGINIA
Department of Motor Vehicles
1800 Washington Street
Charleston, WV 25305

WISCONSIN
Department of Transportation
P O Box 7918
Madison, WI 53707

WYOMING
Department of Revenue
122 West 25th Street
Cheyenne, WY 82002

PUERTO RICO
Department of Transportation
and Public Works
P O Box 41243
Minillar Station
Santurce, PR 00940

MOTOR VEHICLE REGISTRATION OFFICES

To obtain someone's address from an automobile license, registration or title you can contact the appropriate state office below. This service usually requires a fee. Check with the office for further information.

ALABAMA
Title Section
2721 Gunter Park Drive
P O Box 1331
Montgomery, AL 36102
(205) 271-3250

ALASKA
Department of Public Safety
Motor Vehicle Division
Attn: Research
5700 East Tudor Road
Anchorage, AK 99507

ARKANSAS
Office of Motor Vehicles
P O Box 1272
Little Rock, AR 72203

ARIZONA
Motor Vehicle Division
Title Records
1801 W. Jefferson Avenue
Phoenix, AZ 85007

CALIFORNIA
State of California
Department of Motor Vehicles
P O Box 944247
Sacramento, CA 94244-2470
(916) 732-7243

COLORADO
Title Section
140 West 6th Avenue
Denver, CO 80204
(303) 620-4108

CONNECTICUT
Division of Motor Vehicles
60 State Street
Wethersfiield, CT 06109
(203) 566-4410

DELAWARE
Division of Motor Vehicles
Attn: Correspondence Pool
P O Box 698
Dover, DE 19903
(302) 736-3147

DISTRICT OF COLUMBIA
Bureau of Motor Vehicle Services
301 C Street N.W.
Washington, DC 20001
(202) 727-6680

FLORIDA
Division of Motor Vehicles
Neil Kirman Building
Tallahassee, FL 32301
(904) 488-4127

GEORGIA
Motor Vehicle Division
126 Trinity-Washington Bldg
Atlanta, GA 30334
(404) 656-4100

HAWAII
Division of Motor Vehicle Lic.
1455 South Beretania Street
Honolulu, HI 96814
(808) 955-8221

IDAHO
Idaho Transportation Department
Vehicle Research
Box 34
Boise, ID 83707
(208) 334-8663

ILLINOIS
Secretary of State
Vehicle Records Inquiry Sec.
4th Floor, Centennial Bldg
Springfield, IL 62756
(217) 782-6992

INDIANA
Bureau of Motor Vehicles
401 State Office Building
100 North Senate Avenue
Indianapolis, IN 46204
(317) 232-2798

IOWA
Department of Transportation
Office of Vehicle Registration
Lucas State Office Building
Des Moines, IA 50319
(515) 281-7710

KANSAS
Department of Revenue
Division of Vehicles
State Office Building
Topeka, KS 66626
(913) 296-3621

KENTUCKY
Department of Vehicle Reg.
Motor Vehicle Licensing
New State Office Building
Frankfort, KY 40622
(502) 564-7570

LOUISIANA
Office of Motor Vehicles
Department of Public Safety
P O Box 64886
Baton Rouge, LA 70896
(504) 925-6146

MAINE
Department of State
Motor Vehicle Division
State House Station 29
Augusta, ME 04333
(207) 289-3071

MARYLAND
Motor Vehicle Administration
6601 Ritchie Highway, N.E.
Glen Burnie, MD 21062
(301) 768-7000

MASSACHUSETTS
Registrar of Motor Vehicles
100 Nashua Street
Boston, MA 02114
(617) 727-3700

MICHIGAN
Department of State
Bureau of Driver & Veh. Services
7064 Crowner Drive
Lansing, MI 48918
(517) 322-1166

MINNESOTA
Department of Public Safety
Driver and Vehicle Svc. Div.
Transportation Building
St. Paul, MN 55155
(612) 296-6911

MISSISSIPPI
State Tax Commission
Department of Motor Vehicles
Title Division, PO Box 1140
Jackson, MS 39205
(601) 359-1248

MISSOURI
Motor Vehicle Bureau
P O Box 100
Jefferson City, MO 65701
(314) 751-4509

MONTANA
Registrar's Bureau
925 Main Street
Deer Lodge, MT 58722
(406) 846-1423

NEBRASKA
Department of Motor Vehicles
P O Box 94789
Lincoln, NE 68509
(402) 471-2281

NEVADA
Department of Motor Vehicles
Registration Division
Carson City, NV 89711
(702) 855-5370

NEW HAMPSHIRE
Department of Safety
Division of Motor Vehicles
J H Hayes Building
Concord, NH 03305
(603) 271-2251

NEW JERSEY
Bureau of Office Services
Certified Information Unit
25 South Montgomery Street
Trenton, NJ 08666
(609) 292-4102

NEW MEXICO
Motor Vehicles Division
P O Box 1028
Santa Fe, NM 87504
(505) 827-2173

NEW YORK
Department of Motor Vehicles
Empire Plaza
Albany, NY 12228
(518) 474-2121

NORTH CAROLINA
Vehicle Registration
Division of Motor Vehicles
1100 New Bern Avenue
Raleigh, NC 27697
(919) 733-3025

NORTH DAKOTA
Motor Vehicles Department
Capitol Grounds
Bismark, ND 58505
(701) 224-2725

OHIO
Department of Highway Safty
Bureau of Motor Vehicles
P O Box 16520
Columbus, OH 43216
(614) 752-7500

OKLAHOMA
Motor Vehicle Division
2501 Lincoln Blvd.
Oklahoma City, OK 73194
(405) 521-3221

OREGON
Motor Vehicle Division
1905 Lana Avenue, N.E.
Salem, OR 97314
(503) 371-2200

PENNSYLVANIA
Bureau of Motor Vehicles
Transportation & Safety Building
Harrisburg, PA 17122
(717) 787-3130

RHODE ISLAND
Registrar of Motor Vehicles
State Office Building
Providence, RI 02903
(401) 277-2970

SOUTH CAROLINA
Motor Vehicle Division
Dept of Hwy & Public Trans
Columbia, SC 29216
(803) 737-1114

SOUTH DAKOTA
Department of Revenue
118 West Capitol
Pierre, SD 57501
(605) 773-3541

TENNESSEE
Motor Vehicle Division
500 Daderick Street
Nashville, TN 37242
(615) 741-3101

TEXAS
Motor Vehicle Division
Dept of Hwy & Public Transp.
40th and Jackson Avenue
Austin, TX 78779
(512) 465-7611

UTAH
State Tax Commission
Motor Vehicle Division
State Fair Grounds
1905 Motor Avenue
Salt Lake City, UT 84416
(801) 538-8300

VERMONT
Department of Motor Vehicles
120 State Street
Montpelier, VT 05603
(802) 828-2000

VIRGINIA
Department of Motor Vehicles
P O Box 27412
Richmond, VA 23269
(804) 367-0523

WASHINGTON
Department of Licensing
P O Box 9909
Olympia, WA 98504
(206) 753-6946

WEST VIRGINIA
Department of Motor Vehicles
State Capitol Complex, Bldg 3
Charleston, WV 25317
(304) 348-3900

WISCONSIN
Registration Files
Wisconsin Dept of Transp.
P O Box 7909
Madison, WI 53707
(608) 266-1466

WYOMING
Department of Revenue
Motor Vehicle Division
122 West 25th Street
Cheyenne, WY 82002
(307) 777-6511

PUERTO RICO
Department of Transp. &
Public Works
Motor Vehicles Area
P O Box 41243
Minillar Station
Santurce, PR 00940
(809) 723-9607

VITAL RECORDS

Provide as much of the following information as possible in order to obtain birth or death records:

1. Full name of person whose record is being requested
2. Sex and race
3. Parents' names, including maiden name of mother
4. Place of birth or death (city or town, county and state; and name of hospital, if any)
5. Purpose of which copy is needed
6. Relationship to person whose record is being requested

Provide as much of the following information as possible in order to obtain marriage records:
1. Full names of bride and groom (including nicknames)
2. Residence addresses at time of marriage
3. Ages at time of marriage (or dates of birth)
4. Month, day and year of marriage
5. Place of marriage (city or town, county and state)
6. Purpose for which copy is needed
7. Relationship to person whose record is being requested

Provide as much of the following information as possible in order to obtain divorce records:
1. Full names of husband and wife (including nicknames)
2. Present residence address
3. Former addresses (as in court records)
4. Ages at time of divorce (or dates of birth)
5. Date of divorce or annulment
6. Place of divorce or annulment
7. Type of final decree
8. Purpose for which copy is needed
9. Relationship to person whose record is being requested

Below are the addresses of the offices where copies of birth, death, marriage and divorce records can be obtained. Also listed are the charges required by each state.

ALABAMA
Bureau of Vital Statistics
State Department of Health
Montgomery, AL 36130
($5.00)

ALASKA
Bureau of Vital Statistics
Department of Health &
Social Services Pouch H-02G
Juneau, AK 99811
($5.00)

AMERICAN SAMOA
Registrar of Vital Statistics
Vital Statistics Division
Government of Amer Samoa
Pago Pago, AS 96799
($2.00)

ARIZONA
Vital Records Section
Arizona Department of
Health Services
P O Box 3887
Phoenix, AZ 85030
($5.00)

ARKANSAS
Division of Vital Records
Arkansas Dep of Health Svc
4815 West Markham Street
Little Rock, AR 72201
($5.00)

CALIFORNIA
Vital Statistics Branch
Department of Health Svc
410 "N" Street
Sacramento, CA 95814
($11.00)

CANAL ZONE
Panama Canal Commission
Vital Statistics Clerk
APO, Miami 34011
($2.00)

COLORADO
Vital Records Section
Colorado Dept of Health
4210 East 11th Avenue
Denver, CO 80220
($10.00)

CONNECTICUT
Vital Statistics Section
State Dept of Health Svc
Division of Health Statistics
79 Elm Street
Hartford, CT 06115
($3.00)

DELAWARE
Bureau of Vital Statistics
Division of Public Health
State Health Building
Dept of Health & Social Svc
Dover, DE 19901
($5.00)

DISTRICT OF COLUMBIA
Vital Records Branch
615 Pennsylvania Ave N.W.
Washington, DC 20004
($5.00)

FLORIDA
Dept of Health Rehab Svc
Office Vital Statistics
P O Box 210
Jacksonville, FL 32231
($6.50)

GEORGIA
Georgia Dept of Human Svc
Vital Records Unit
Room 217-H
47 Trinity Ave, SW
Atlanta, GA 30334
($3.00)

GUAM
Office of Vital Statistics
Dept of Public Health &
Social Svc
P O Box 2816
Government of Guam
Agana, GU 96910 ($2.00)

HAWAII
Research and Statistics Office
State Dept of Health
P O Box 3378
Honolulu, HI 96801
($2.00)

IDAHO
Bureau of Vital Statistics
Standard & Local Health Svc
State Dept of Health & Welfare
Statehouse
Boise, ID 83720 ($6.00)

ILLINOIS
Office of Vital Records
State Dept of Public Health
535 W Jefferson Street
Springfield, IL 62761
($10.00)

INDIANA
Division of Vital Records
State Board of Health
1330 West Michigan Street
Indianapolis, IN 46206
($6.00)

IOWA
Iowa State Dept of Health
Vital Records Section
Lucas State Office Building
Des Moines, IA 50319
($6.00)

KANSAS
Bureau of Registration & Health
Kansas Dept of Health &
Environment
6700 S Topeka Avenue
Topeka, KS 66620
($6.00)

KENTUCKY
Office of Vital Statistics
Dept of Human Resources
275 East Main Street
Frankfort, KY 40621
($5.00)

LOUISIANA
Division of Vital Records
Office of Health Services &
Environment Quality
P O Box 60630
New Orleans, LA 70160
($8.00)

MAINE
Office of Vital Records
Human Services Building
Station 2
State House
Augusta, ME 04333
($5.00)

MARYLAND
Division of Vital Records
State Dept of Health &
Mental Hygiene
State Office Building
P O Box 13146
201 W Preston Street
Baltimore, MD 21203
($3.00)

MASSACHUSETTS
Registry of Vital Records &
Statistics
State Dept of Health
Room 105 McCormack Bldg
1 Ashburton Place
Boston, MA 02108
($3.00)

MICHIGAN
Office of Vital Statistics &
Health
Michigan Dept of Public
Health
3500 North Logan Street
Lansing, MI 48914
($10.00)

MINNESOTA
Minnesota Dept of Health
Section of Vital Statistics
717 Delaware Street, NE
Minneapolis, MN 55440
($7.00)

MISSISSIPPI
Bureau of Vital Records
State Board of Health
P O Box 1700
Jackson, MS 39205
($10.00)

MISSOURI
Division of Health
Bureau of Vital Records
State Department of Health &
Welfare
Jefferson City, MO 65101
($5.00)

MONTANA
Bureau of Records & Stats
State Dept of Health &
Environmental Sciences
Helena, MT 59601
($4.00)

NEBRASKA
Bureau of Vital Statistics
State Department of Health
301 N Centennial Mall South
P O Box 95007
Lincoln, NE 68509
($6.00)

NEVADA
Division of Health Vital Stats
Capital Complex
Carson City, NV 89710
($6.00)

NEW HAMPSHIRE
Bureau of Vital Records
Health & Welfare Building
Hazel Drive
Concord, NH 03301
($3.00)

NEW JERSEY
State Department of Health
Bureau of Vital Statistics
CN360
Trenton, NJ 08625
($4.00)

NEW MEXICO
Vital Statistics Bureau
New Mexico Health Svc Div
P O Box 968
Santa Fe, NM 87503
($4.00)

NEW YORK
Bureau of Vital Records
State Department of Health
Empire State Plaza
Tower Building
Albany, NY 12237
($5.00)

NORTH CAROLINA
Bureau of Vital Statistics
Dept of Human Resources
Division of Health Services
Vital Records Branch
P O Box 2091
Raleigh, NC 27602
($5.00)

NORTH DAKOTA
Division of Vital Records
State Department of Health
Office of Statistical Services
Bismarck, ND 58505
($5.00)

OHIO
Division of Vital Statistics
Ohio Department of Health
G-20 Ohio Depts Building
65 S Front Street
Columbus, OH 43215
($7.00)

OKLAHOMA
Vital Records Section
State Department of Health
NE Tenth St & Stonewall
P O Box 53551
Oklahoma City, OK 73152
($5.00)

OREGON
Oregon State Health Division
Vital Statistics Section
P O Box 116
Portland, OR 97207
($5.00)

PENNSYLVANIA
Division of Vital Statistics
State Department of Health
Central Building
101 South Mercer Street
P O Box 1528
New Castle, PA 16103
($4.00)

PUERTO RICO
Division of Demographic
Registry & Vital Statistics
Department of Health
San Juan, PR 00908
($2.00)

RHODE ISLAND
Division of Vital Statistics
State Department of Health
Room 101 Cannon Building
75 Davis Street
Providence, RI 02908
($5.00)

SOUTH CAROLINA
Office of Vital Records &
Public Health
S Carolina Dept of Health &
Environmental Control
2600 Bull Street
Columbia, SC 29201
($5.00)

SOUTH DAKOTA
Bureau of Vital Statistics
State Department of Health
Health Statistics Program
Joe Foss Office Building
Pierre, SD 57501
($5.00)

TENNESSEE
Division of Vital Records
State Dept of Public Health
Cordell Hull Building
Nashville, TN 37219
($6.00)

UTAH
Bureau of Health Statistics
Utah Department of Health
150 W North Temple
P O Box 2500
Salt Lake City, UT 84110
($10.00)

VIRGINIA
Division of Vital Records &
Health Statistics
State Dept of Health
James Madison Building
P O Box 1000
Richmond, VA 23208
($5.00)

VIRGIN ISLANDS-
ST. CROIX
Registrar of Vital Statistics
Charles Harwood Memorial
Hospital
St. Croix, VI 00802
($5.00)

WEST VIRGINIA
Division of Vital Statistics
State Department of Health
State Office Building No. 3
Charleston, WV 25305
($5.00)

TEXAS
Bureau of Vital Statistics
Texas Department of Health
1100 W 49th Street
Austin, TX 78756
($5.00)

VERMONT
Vermont Dept of Health
Vital Records Section
Box 70
115 Colchester Avenue
Burlington, VT 05401
($5.00)

VIRGIN ISLANDS-
ST. THOMAS
Registrar of Vital Statistics
Charlotte Amalie
St. Thomas, VI 00802
($5.00)

WASHINGTON
Vital Records
P O Box 9709, LB11
Olympia, WA 98504
($6.00)

WISCONSIN
Bureau of Health Statistics
Wisconsin Division of Health
P O Box 309
Madison, WI 53701
($7.00)

WYOMING
Vital Records Services
Div of Health & Medical Svc
Hathaway Building
Cheyenne, WY 82002
($5.00)

OVERSEAS BIRTHS
Authentication Office
21st St & Virginia Ave NW
Washington, DC 20025
($3.00)

TRUST TERRITORY OF
THE PACIFIC ISLANDS
Director, Medical Services
Department of Medical Svc
Saipan Marinas Isld 96950
($.10 per 100 words)
Make Check to "Clerk of Court"
Air Mail postage suggested

OVERSEAS BIRTHS
PASSPORT SERVICES
State Department
Washington, DC 20524
($4.00)

CHAPTER TEN

IF THE PERSON YOU ARE TRYING TO LOCATE IS DECEASED

This chapter provides addresses of government and private organizations that may be able to tell you if the person you are looking is deceased. If also explains how to get casualty reports and to find out where a military veteran is buried.

TO DETERMINE THROUGH THE SOCIAL SECURITY ADMINISTRATION IF AN INDIVIDUAL IS DECEASED

The Social Security Administration will tell you if an individual is deceased, if you provide them with a SSN. Contact:

Department Of Health and Human Resources
Social Security Administration   (800) 234-5772
Albuquerque Teleservice Center
Post Office Box 27170
Albuquerque, New Mexico 87125-7170

TO DETERMINE THROUGH THE DEPARTMENT OF VETERANS AFFAIRS IF A VETERAN IS DECEASED

The VA will tell you if a veteran is deceased if they can identify him in their files. They can also give you his date of death and place of burial, if known. The VA is informed of veterans death by funeral homes, family members and some government agencies and have excellent records in this regard. Call any VA regional office for assistance (see chapter five for details and telephone numbers).

THE NATIONAL DEATH INDEX SERVICE

Cambridge Statistical Research Associates, Inc. (CSRA) is a firm based in Cambridge, Ohio which provides a National Death Index service. The Index is compiled from available government sources, mainly the Social Security Administration, and currently consists of over forty-two million death records, updated quarterly. The majority of these deaths occurred after 1962. Over 85% of all decedents after 1962 can be found in this Index. The remaining 15% are most likely persons who never participated in the Social Security System due to either their age at death, or occupation. The percentage of deaths covered by the Index will improve in time as more government databases are incorporated, and since almost all Americans are now included in the Social Security System.

The Death Index for each decedent consists of the following items: Social Security number, last and first names, dates of birth and death, state of residence, and ZIP codes to which benefits, if any, were sent. The search process is highly flexible. Generally, only the first and last names are needed for a search. However, if the last name is very common, an approximate year of birth or death may be necessary. In special cases, searches may also be conducted based on various combinations of data such as a first name with a precise date of birth, or a name limited to a certain geographical location. Of course, if available, the most direct input is an accurate Social Security number.

CSRA Inc. is offering the search service to the general public on both a subscription and non-subscription basis. Requests may be submitted by mail, phone, or Fax. The normal turn-around is one working day. On-line service is also available. The cost per search is $6.00 by mail with a self-addressed stamped envelope or $8.00 by phone or Fax. Visa or Mastercard is accepted.

Cambridge Statistical Research   (614) 432-6400
Associates, Inc.
760 Wheeling Avenue
Cambridge, OH 43725

TO LOCATE NEXT OF KIN OF MILITARY CASUALTIES

You may write to the appropriate armed service for assistance if you wish to contact the next of kin of military members who were casualties during recent wars. Names and addresses of next of kin are contained on all casualty reports.

Headquarters, U.S. Marine Corps   (703) 640-3939
Casualty Branch MMRB-10
Quantico, VA 22134-0001

Air Force Military Personnel Center,
AFMPC/DPMC
Randolph Air Force Base, Texas 78150-6001

Department of the Navy, NMPC-122
Casualty Assistance Branch
Washington, D.C. 20370-5120

Director, Army Casualty and Memorial
Affairs Operation Center
Total Army Personnel Agency, DAPC-PED
2461 Eisenhower Avenue
Alexandria, VA 22331

TO LOCATE GRAVESITES OF US SERVICEMEN BURIED OVERSEAS

The American Battle Monuments Commission (ABMC) can provide names of 124,912 US war dead of World War I and II who are interned in American burial grounds in foreign countries. The ABMC also can provide the names of any of 94,093 US servicemen and women who were missing in action or lost or buried at sea during the World Wars, the Korean and Viet Nam Wars. For further information contact:

The American Battle Monuments Commission
Casemir Pulaski Building   (202) 272-0533
20 Massachusetts Ave. N.W.   (202) 272-0532
Washington, DC 20314-0300

TO LOCATE GRAVESITES OF VETERANS AND THEIR DEPENDENTS BURIED IN VA CEMETERIES

For information concerning veterans and their dependents who are buried in VA cemeteries contact:

Department of Veterans Affairs
National Cemetery System
Washington, D.C. 20420

TO OBTAIN COPIES OF MILITARY CASUALTY REPORTS

ARMY CASUALTIES

The Casualty Information System for the periods 1961-1981 contains records of casualties suffered by all US Army personnel and their dependents. Extracts of records for all US Army Active Duty personnel who have died are available from the following:

Center for Electronic Records (NNX)   (202) 501-5579
National Archives and Records Administration
Washington, DC 20408

Individual Deceased Personnel Files, 1943-1960, 1965-1971, 1973-1980, 1982-1985. Documents relating to the death, recovery or non-recovery of body, funeral arrangements and burial location. Contact:

Military Reference Branch (NNRM-S)   (202) 501-5385
National Archives
Washington National Records Center
Washington, DC 20409

CASUALTIES OF ALL MILITARY SERVICES

Vietnam Conflict Casualty List of all servicemen who died as a result of hostile actions or from other causes. Also includes MIA's and POW's. Contact:

Center for Electronic Records (NNX)   (202) 501-5579
National Archives and Records Administration
Washington, DC 20408

NAVY AND MARINE CORPS CASUALTIES

Casualty records covering 1942 to present (Marine Corps) and World War II to present (Navy), containing names and service numbers of personnel who are deceased or missing and those injured in a battle zone. Contact:

Commandant of the Marine Corps   (703) 640-3939
Headquarters, US Marine Corps
Casualty Branch MMRB-10
Quantico, VA 22134-0001

or:

Naval Military Personnel Command   (703) 614-3654
Department of the Navy   (703) 614-2983
Washington, DC 20370

TO LOCATE FAMILIES AND FRIENDS OF DECEASED VIETNAM VETERANS

"In Touch" is a locator service whose main goal is to connect Vietnam veterans and the families of those who died in Vietnam. Many Vietnam veterans need to locate the families of their fallen comrades to share memories, anecdotes, pictures, tapes, etc. or just to keep a 20 year old promise to their lost buddy or to themselves.

At the same time, families are trying to find fellow veterans of their loved ones who were lost in Vietnam. And the children of those who were lost in Vietnam want to talk to their fathers' comrades to learn what their fathers were like when they were the ages many of their children are now. Sons and daughters, siblings, widows, and parents are also connecting with each other through this program.

In cooperation with other locator services, "In Touch" also helps Vietnam veterans find each other. There is no charge for any "In Touch" service which are sponsored by Friend of the Vietnam Veterans Memorial, a non-profit, largely volunteer organization whose purpose is to continue the healing effects begun by the building of the Vietnam Veterans Memorial.

"In Touch"   (202) 628-0726
Friends of VN Vet Memorial
1224 M St NW
Washington, DC 20005

TO LOCATE CHILDREN OF WORLD WAR II CASUALTIES

The American World War II Orphans Network is searching for sons and daughters of soldiers who were killed or missing in World War II. They are also attempting to locate every memorial across the United States which lists World War II veterans. The Network would like to hear from everyone who knows about the existence of a memorial in their town or neighborhood. They would also like to hear from every person who lost a father in World War II.

American World War II Orphans Network   (206) 733-1678
PO Box 4359
Bellingham, WA 98227

CHAPTER ELEVEN

CONCLUSION

Now that you have read this book, you should realize there are many methods available to locate people who are or have been in the military. It may take more than one attempt to be successful, but if you are persistent, you will ultimately find the person you are trying to locate.

If you have any questions or problems concerning this book, write to the author, Lt. Col. Richard S. Johnson at the address below. We would also appreciate hearing about any successful searches.

Since the information contained in this book changes at times, revised editions will be published periodically. If you have any comments that may improve future copies of this book they will certainly be appreciated. Please write us at the following address:

MILITARY INFORMATION ENTERPRISES
P O BOX 340081
FORT SAM HOUSTON, TEXAS 78234

GLOSSARY

ARCHIVES
The depositories of historical documents of the Federal Government. The National Personnel Records Center is part of the Archives.

ARMED FORCES
The Armed Forces are composed of the Army, Navy, Marine Corps, Air Force and the Coast Guard.

DEPARTMENT OF VETERANS AFFAIRS
The Department of Veterans Affairs is the new name for the Veterans Administration. The abbreviation VA is used in this book.

FREEDOM OF INFORMATION ACT OF 1974
Federal law requiring US government agencies and the Armed Forces to release records to the public on request unless information is exempted by the Privacy Act or for national security reasons.

LOCATOR
An office or organization that has names, SSN, and units of assignment of all military personnel assigned to a particular installation.

MERCHANT MARINES
The civilian Maritime Fleet.

PRIVACY ACT OF 1974
Federal law designed to protect an individual constitutional right to privacy. The law also provide disclosure to an individual of information that the federal government maintains on that individual.

RANK
The grade or rating an individual holds in his military organization.

RESERVE COMPONENTS
The Reserve Components include the Army, Navy, Air Force, Marine Corps, Coast Guard reserve and the Army and Air Force National Guard.

RETIRED MILITARY MEMBER
A person who has completed twenty or more years of duty in any of the military components is entitled to retired pay. He may be retired from an active or reserve component of a service (a member of the Reserve Components is not eligible for retired pay until age 60). A military member may be retired from active duty for disability due to injury or illness with less than 20 years of active service.

SERVICE NUMBER
A number formerly used by the armed forces to identify individual members. The SSN is now used in place of the service number. The Army and Air Force discontinued using service numbers on July 1, 1969, The Navy and Marine Corps on July 1, 1972 and the Coast Guard on October 1, 1974.

SOCIAL SECURITY NUMBER
The nine digit number that is used by the Uniformed Services to identify individual members.

THE UNIFORMED SERVICES
Composed of the Armed Forces, the Public Health Service, and the National Oceanic and Atmospheric Administration.

VA
This abbreviation refers to The Department of Veterans Affairs.

VETERAN
A person who has served on active duty in one or more of the Armed Services.

WORLD WIDE LOCATOR
An office or organization operated by each of the Uniformed Services which maintains the name, rank, unit assignment and world wide location of members of their perspective service.

INDEX

INDIVIDUAL DATA WORKSHEET

NAME: _____

PARENT'S NAME:_____
DATE AND PLACE OF
BIRTH:_____

SOCIAL SECURITY NUMBER: _____ - _____ - _____

SERVICE NUMBER:_____
VA FILE OR CLAIM
NUMBER: _____
BRANCH OF
SERVICE: _____
DATES OF MILITARY
SERVICE: _____
UNITS
ASSIGNED/DATES: _____
BASE/POST/INSTALLATIONS
ASSIGNED/DATES: _____
FORMER MAILING
ADDRESS:_____
MEMBERSHIP IN RESERVES OR NATIONAL
GUARD: _____
                (UNITS AND DATES)
CHURCH
AFFILIATION: _____
DRIVER'S
LICENSE: _____
          (NUMBER)   (STATE)
MEMBERSHIP IN CLUBS, LODGES AND CIVIC
ORGANIZATIONS:_____
NAMES AND LOCATION OF SCHOOLS
ATTENDED: _____

_____

SPOUSE'S NAME: _____
          (MAIDEN NAME, DATE AND PLACE OF MARRIAGE)
CHILDREN'S
NAMES:_____
          (PLACES AND DATES OF BIRTH)

OTHER PUBLICATIONS AVAILABLE

LIFELINE: THE ACTION GUIDE TO ADOPTION SEARCH by Virgil L. Klunder This publication is the most valuable guide available in conducting an successful adoption search. It is a unique resource for all adoptees, birthparents and adoptive parents. It contains 409 pages of the latest search techniques along with 59 sample letters, documents and checklists covering all 50 states and 14 countries. This book gives a detailed 21 point directory of vital search resources for every state; including current laws, records data/costs, inside tips and instruction from local search experts and much more. It includes over 1,000 updated names, addresses, and telephone numbers of public and private organizations used daily by searchers 409 pages $28.00

AMERICAN MEDALS AND DECORATIONS A complete guide to the decorations and awards of the United States from 1782 to the present by Evans E. Kerrigan illustrated 242 pages $28.00

HOW TO FIND ANYONE ANYWHERE by Ralph D. Thomas Secret sources and techniques for locating missing persons, 62 pages
$22.00

HOW TO INVESTIGATE BY COMPUTER by Ralph D. Thomas A manual of the new investigative technology that gives you the sources and teaches you to investigate by computer. Learn about hard-to-find sources of information and how to access them, 102 pages
$41.00

MILITARY REUNION HANDBOOK by Bill Masciangelo and Tom Ninkovich Military Reunion Handbook A Guide For Reunion Planners is a step by step manual for reunion organizers that deals with every aspect of military reunions. This 214 page book was written by Bill Masciangelo and Tom Ninkovich who are the two most knowledgeable people in the country on planning and conducting a reunion. This book is an absolute must for every reunion association whether they are planning their first or fiftieth reunion $16.00

ORDER FORM
Military Information Enterprises
PO Box 340081
Ft. Sam Houston, TX 78234
(512) 828-4054

We Accept Government Purchase Orders.

PUBLICATION	PRICE	QTY	AMT
How To Locate Anyone Who is or Has Been in The Military	$16.00		
Other books desired			

Prices include postage and handling   TOTAL: $____

Texas Orders Please
add 8% Sales Tax. $____
For 1st Class Mail please add $2.00 per book.
Consult Publisher for International Mail Prices. $____

Total Amount Enclosed: $____

Mastercard, Visa, American Express   Card #_____

Expiration Date __/__/__

Signature_____

Name:_____

Street/Apt no:_____

City/State/Zip_____

Telephone:(___)_____   Please remit entire order form.

REQUEST PERTAINING TO MILITARY RECORDS

Please read instructions on the reverse. If more space is needed, use plain paper.

SECTION I — INFORMATION NEEDED TO LOCATE RECORDS (Furnish as much as possible)

1. NAME USED DURING SERVICE (Last, first, and middle)	2. SOCIAL SECURITY NO.	3. DATE OF BIRTH	4. PLACE OF BIRTH

5. ACTIVE SERVICE, PAST AND PRESENT (For an effective records search, it is important that ALL service be shown below)

BRANCH OF SERVICE (Also, show last organization, if known)	DATES OF ACTIVE SERVICE		Check one		SERVICE NUMBER DURING THIS PERIOD
	DATE ENTERED	DATE RELEASED	OFFICER	ENLISTED	

6. RESERVE SERVICE, PAST OR PRESENT   If "none," check here ▶ ☐

a. BRANCH OF SERVICE	b. DATES OF MEMBERSHIP		c. Check one		d. SERVICE NUMBER DURING THIS PERIOD
	FROM	TO	OFFICER ☐	ENLISTED ☐	

7. NATIONAL GUARD MEMBERSHIP   (Check one):   ☐ a. ARMY   ☐ b. AIR FORCE   ☐ c. NONE

d. STATE	e. ORGANIZATION	f. DATES OF MEMBERSHIP		g. Check one		h. SERVICE NUMBER DURING THIS PERIOD
		FROM	TO	OFFICER ☐	ENLISTED ☐	

8. IS SERVICE PERSON DECEASED   ☐ YES   ☐ NO   If "yes," enter date of death.

9. IS (WAS) INDIVIDUAL A MILITARY RETIREE OR FLEET RESERVIST   ☐ YES   ☐ NO

SECTION II — REQUEST

1. EXPLAIN WHAT INFORMATION OR DOCUMENTS YOU NEED; OR, CHECK ITEM 2; OR, COMPLETE ITEM 3

2. IF YOU ONLY NEED A STATEMENT OF SERVICE check here ☐

3. LOST SEPARATION DOCUMENT REPLACEMENT REQUEST (Complete a or b, and c.)

	a. REPORT OF SEPARATION ☐ (DD Form 214 or equivalent)	YEAR ISSUED	This contains information normally needed to determine eligibility for benefits. It may be furnished only to the veteran, the surviving next of kin, or to a representative with veteran's signed release (item 5 of this form).
	b. DISCHARGE ☐ CERTIFICATE	YEAR ISSUED	This shows only the date and character at discharge. It is of little value in determining eligibility for benefits. It may be issued only to veterans discharged honorably or under honorable conditions; or, if deceased, to the surviving spouse.

c. EXPLAIN HOW SEPARATION DOCUMENT WAS LOST

4. EXPLAIN PURPOSE FOR WHICH INFORMATION OR DOCUMENTS ARE NEEDED

6. REQUESTER

a. IDENTIFICATION (check appropriate box)

☐ Same person identified in Section I   ☐ Surviving spouse

☐ Next of kin (relationship) _____

☐ Other (specify)

b. SIGNATURE (see instruction 3 on reverse side)   DATE OF REQUEST

5. RELEASE AUTHORIZATION, IF REQUIRED (Read instruction 3 on reverse side)

I hereby authorize release of the requested information/documents to the person indicated at right (item 7).

VETERAN SIGN HERE ▶

(If signed by other than veteran show relationship to veteran.)

7. Please type or print clearly —   COMPLETE RETURN ADDRESS

Name, number and street, city, State and ZIP code

TELEPHONE NO. (include area code) ▶

180-106   NSN 7540-00-142-9360   STANDARD FORM 180 (Rev.) Prescribed by NARA (36 CFR 1228)

INSTRUCTIONS

1. Information needed to locate records. Certain identifying information is necessary to determine the location of an individual's record of military service. Please give careful consideration to and answer each item on this form. If you do not have and cannot obtain the information for an item, show "NA," meaning the information is "not available." Include as much of the requested information as you can. This will help us to give you the best possible service.

2. Charges for service. A nominal fee is charged for certain types of service. In most instances service fees cannot be determined in advance. If your request involves a service fee you will be notified as soon as that determination is made.

3. Restrictions on release of information. Information from records of military personnel is released subject to restrictions imposed by the military departments consistent with the provisions of the Freedom of Information Act of 1967 (as amended in 1974) and the Privacy Act of 1974. A service person has access to almost any information contained in his own record. The next of kin, if the veteran is deceased, and Federal officers for official purposes, are authorized to receive information from a military service or medical record only as specified in the above cited Acts. Other requesters must have the release authorization, in item 5 of the form, signed by the veteran or, if deceased, by the next of kin. Employers

and others needing proof of military service are expected to accept the information shown on documents issued by the Armed Forces at the time a service person is separated.

4. Location of military personnel records. The various categories of military personnel records are described in the chart below. For each category there is a code number which indicates the address at the bottom of the page to which this request should be sent. For each military service there is a note explaining approximately how long the records are held by the military service before they are transferred to the National Personnel Records Center, St. Louis. Please read these notes carefully and make sure you send your inquiry to the right address. Please note especially that the record is not sent to the National Personnel Records Center as long as the person retains any sort of reserve obligation, whether drilling or non-drilling.

(If the person has two or more periods of service within the same branch, send your request to the office having the record for the last period of service.)

5. Definitions for abbreviations used below:
NPRC—National Personnel Records Center   PERS—Personnel Records
TDRL—Temporary Disability Retirement List   MED—Medical Records

SERVICE	NOTE: (See paragraph 4 above.)	CATEGORY OF RECORDS — WHERE TO WRITE		ADDRESS CODE ▼
AIR FORCE (USAF)	Except for TDRL and general officers retired with pay, Air Force records are transferred to NPRC from Code 1, 90 days after separation and from Code 2, 150 days after separation.	Active members (includes National Guard on active duty in the Air Force), TDRL, and general officers retired with pay		1
		Reserve, retired reservist in nonpay status, current National Guard officers not on active duty in Air Force, and National Guard released from active duty in Air Force.		2
		Current National Guard enlisted not on active duty in Air Force.		13
		Discharged, deceased, and retired with pay.		14
COAST GUARD (USCG)	Coast Guard officer and enlisted records are transferred to NPRC 7 months after separation.	Active, reserve, and TDRL members.		3
		Discharged, deceased, and retired members *(see next item).*		14
		Officers separated before 1/1/29 and enlisted personnel separated before 1/1/15.		6
MARINE CORPS (USMC)	Marine Corps records are transferred to NPRC between 6 and 9 months after separation.	Active, TDRL, and Selected Marine Corps Reserve members.		4
		Individual Ready Reserve and Fleet Marine Corps Reserve members.		5
		Discharged, deceased, and retired members *(see next item).*		14
		Members separated before 1/1/1905.		6
ARMY (USA)	Army records are transferred to NPRC as follows: Active Army and Individual Ready Reserve Control Groups: About 60 days after separation. U.S. Army Reserve Troop Unit personnel: About 120 to 180 days after separation.	Reserve, living retired members, retired general officers, and active duty records of current National Guard members who performed service in the U.S. Army before 7/1/72.*		7
		Active officers (including National Guard on active duty in the U.S. Army).		8
		Active enlisted (including National Guard on active duty in the U.S. Army) and enlisted TDRL.		9
		Current National Guard officers not on active duty in the U.S. Army.		12
		Current National Guard enlisted not on active duty in the U.S. Army.		13
		Discharged and deceased members *(see next item).*		14
		Officers separated before 7/1/17 and enlisted separated before 11/1/12.		6
		Officers and warrant officers TDRL.		8
NAVY (USN)	Navy records are transferred to NPRC 6 months after retirement or complete separation.	Active members (including reservists on duty)—PERS and MED		10
		Discharged, deceased, retired (with and without pay) less than six months, TDRL, drilling and nondrilling reservists	PERS ONLY	10
			MED ONLY	11
		Discharged, deceased, retired (with and without pay) more than six months *(see next item)*—PERS & MED		14
		Officers separated before 1/1/03 and enlisted separated before 1/1/1886—PERS and MED		6

Code 12 applies to active duty records of current National Guard officers who performed service in the U.S. Army after 6/30/72.
Code 13 applies to active duty records of current National Guard enlisted members who performed service in the U.S. Army after 6/30/72.

ADDRESS LIST OF CUSTODIANS (BY CODE NUMBERS SHOWN ABOVE)—Where to write / send this form for each category of records

1	Air Force Manpower and Personnel Center Military Personnel Records Division Randolph AFB, TX 78150-6001	**5**	Marine Corps Reserve Support Center 10950 El Monte Overland Park, KS 66211-1408	**8**	USA MILPERCEN ATTN: DAPC-MSR 200 Stovall Street Alexandria, VA 22332-0400	**12** Army National Guard Personnel Center Columbia Pike Office Building 5600 Columbia Pike Falls Church, VA 22041
2	Air Reserve Personnel Center Denver, CO 80280-5000	**6**	Military Archives Division National Archives and Records Administration Washington, DC 20408	**9**	Commander U.S. Army Enlisted Records and Evaluation Center Ft. Benjamin Harrison, IN 46249-5301	**13** The Adjutant General *(of the appropriate State, DC, or Puerto Rico)*
3	Commandant U.S. Coast Guard Washington, DC 20593-0001	**7**	Commander U.S. Army Reserve Personnel Center ATTN: DARP-PAS 9700 Page Boulevard St. Louis, MO 63132-5200	**10**	Commander Naval Military Personnel Command ATTN: NMPC-036 Washington, DC 20370-5036	**14** National Personnel Records Center *(Military Personnel Records)* 9700 Page Boulevard St. Louis, MO 63132
4	Commandant of the Marine Corps (Code MMRB-10) Headquarters, U.S. Marine Corps Washington, DC 20380-0001			**11**	Naval Reserve Personnel Center New Orleans, LA 70146-5000	

490-498 (m)

STANDARD FORM 180 BACK (Rev 7-86)